HIP HOP

×

FINAN¢E

HIP HOP
×
FINAN¢E

BY DREW BOYER CFP®

FOREWORD BY
'DOWNTOWN' JOSH BROWN

LEFT HAND WRITES PUBLISHING

Left Hand Writes Publishing
679-G High St.
Worthington
Ohio
43085
United States

Tel: +1-(614) 226-8569
Email: press@hiphopxfinance.com
Website: www.hiphopxfinance.com

First Published in 2025
Copyright © Drew W. Boyer

The right of Drew W. Boyer to be identified as the Author has been asserted in accordance with the Copyright, Design, and Patents Act of 1988.

Paperback ISBN: 979-8-9920248-1-4
Hardcover ISBN: 979-8-9920248-0-7
Hardcover B+W ISBN: 979-8-9920248-4-5
eBook ISBN: 979-8-9920248-2-1
Audiobook ISBN: 979-8-9920248-3-8

All images used in this publication have been licensed exclusviely through: Depositphotos Inc.,115 West 30th Street, Suite 1110B, New York, NY, 10001, United States.

While every effort has been made to ensure that information in this book is accurate, no liability can be accepted for any loss incurred in any way whatsoever by any person relying solely on the information contained herein.

No responsiblity for loss occasionaed to any person or corporate body acting or refraining to act as a result of reading material in this book can be accepted byt the Publisher, by the Author, or by the employees of the Author.

This Publisher does not have any control over or any responsibility for any Author's or third-party websites referred to in or on this book.

For Johanna, Lena, and Elise.

TRACK LIST

FOREWORD

In 1986 I was nine years old, away from home at summer camp for the first time. One of the boys in my bunk had a boombox and he played cassette tapes while we did our daily chores - sweeping, putting away the laundry, mopping the bathroom, emptying the trash bins. Lots of different music came out of his speakers from one day to the next, from Madonna to Steve Winwood, Kenny Loggins on the Top Gun soundtrack to Whitney Houston's hits from her debut album. But there was one tape that made the rotation every morning. By request. Run-D.M.C.'s "Raising Hell" was in heavy demand. Specifically, the single Peter Piper, which had been released just before the summer began on May 15th.

Most of us had heard some hip hop on the radio and had seen a few videos on TV, but "Raising Hell" was the first record we'd memorized all the words to and played side to side, over and over again. To paraphrase the Notorious B.I.G., we let our tape rock til our tape popped. Literally. We had to ask our parents to bring us some backups when they came up to visit Camp Summit on Visiting Day that July. It became the soundtrack to our summer.

This led me down a rabbit hole of discovering new rap music when I got home that fall. I started buying everything I could get my hands on from the local record stores, Long Island Sound in Merrick, New York and Tower Records in Carle Place. I devoured Public Enemy (they grew up in the town next door in Freeport, Long Island), EPMD (also from Long Island), Eric B. & Rakim, the Digital Underground, Slick Rick, LL Cool J, KRS One and Big Daddy Kane. Most of these artists grew up and lived within a few miles of me. They were my superheroes.

It wasn't until later in life that I realized what was so special about hip hop music relative to all the genres I was listening to. If rock and roll was about defiance, country was about tradition, the blues were about heartache and R&B was about sex, hip hop, at its core, was about ambition. It was about coming from nothing and taking what you wanted. It was about improving one's own situation, by any means necessary, or dying trying. The first major hip hop single, (Rappers Delight), is riddled with lyrics about getting cars, clothes, credit cards and a color TV. This motif of coming up in the world persists even into the modern day, long after the rap industry has become a multi-billion dollar enterprise. Each successive generation of new emcees produces a fresh spin on the original message: Watch me make it, despite all odds.

I internalized this message and it became a part of my persona. I didn't grow up in the South Bronx, or in College Grove, or on 8 Mile or Linden Boulevard. I've never even been to Compton. But I got it then. And I'm still getting it now, forty years later.

'DOWNTOWN' JOSH BROWN

Founder and CEO of Ritholtz Wealth Management
Merrick, New York - December, 2024

INTRO

If you're reading this book, thank you, and welcome to my financial gang! No matter what track you're on in the album of life, you're going to learn how to become a financial gangster, get off "Debt Row", and stack your cashflow.

What's a financial gangster? Per Snoop's iconic line, it's someone who keeps their mind on their money and their money on their mind. It's found at the intersection of hip-hop and finance where we take Jay-Z's "99 Problems" and make sure money isn't one by the end of this book.

How?

I'm going to share the same Blueprint this CERTIFIED FINANCIAL PLANNER®, with over two decades of personal finance experience, has followed and shared with all my clients. I went from being a broke-joke in -$100,000 of bad debt, to becoming a fulfilled, multi-millionaire looking to give back this smart money wisdom. It just takes some hustle, time, and a willingness to graduate from the "School of Hard Knocks". Like it or not, we all get enrolled in after Graduation- just like Kanye.

Are you enrolled there right now? If you're feeling the effects of inflation, unpaid credit card debt, and/or living month-to-month with no way to save, you're like when Drake "Started From the Bottom" . It's not your fault you are being overwhelmed daily by a culture that promotes a spend-to-pretend lifestyle, that leaves you feeling left behind or worse- without financial hope. Let's squash that beef right now.

Chances are you've received no formal financial education and only have learned what you know through trial and error or if you're lucky, a few pieces of advice from your family or friends. That's exactly why I wanted to write this book. I was on Debt Row after making bad money mistakes and had to teach myself how to break out.

Through combining my loves of both music and finance, I want to entertain and educate, but most of all- financially empower you to live a fulfilling and successful life. Whatever that may be to you. My financial gang and I are on a mission- will you join us?

I wrote this book for 18-year-old me whose net worth was some baseball cards, a respectable collection of classic hip-hop cassette tapes, and a bad attitude. He had no idea the amount of bad debt he'd pile up through student loans, credit cards, and family loans by age 25. He also had no idea what a credit score was and why it mattered. Budgeting, taxes, and investing? That's something he overheard his parents talking about at night after he went to bed. He had been shown the ways of hustling and entrepreneurship, that you always pay back a loan, but don't forget to pay it forward by giving back.

I wrote this for my financial gang now, so you all can have the advantage I didn't: an organized, step-by-step financial guide that is sampled from hip-hop's greatest rhymes and minds. That's why I'd like to think younger me would've soaked up this book.

This won't be your typical boring finance book. I'll bet you the price of admission that this is the first personal finance book with a parental advisory sticker on the front. There are witty track "titles" instead of chapters. It's also chalked-full of:

• Your favorite hip-hop rhymes to educate,
• Easy-to-understand charts and graphs to illustrate,
• "Take Action!" boxes at the end of those tracks to motivate, and a
• "Hip Hop X Finance" Spotify™ playlist so that you financial gangsters can move to the music while you stack your cash flow.

The financial lessons are woven in between my own 20-year struggle through personal finance and hip-hop superstars greatest wins and fails. What's not to love? Music! Hardship! Wins and fails. Oh yeah, that finance part… the topic may put many to sleep, but not in these pages.

Those that learn, earn. Remember that!

TRACK 0.

THE COME-UP

TRACK 0: THE COME-UP

On August 11th, 1973, at a back-to-school party in the Bronx, DJ Kool Herc performed what is widely considered the very first hip-hop set. He looped records, extended instrumental breaks so the party could dance longer, and then rapped lyrics and announcements with friends over the beats. It was the start of a new genre of music. One that would grow into a $16 billion global brand just 50 years later.

My fellow Generation X'ers and I got to witness this phenomenon firsthand during the golden age of hip-hop before it became commercialized, formulized, and known for minting billionaires out of rap entrepreneurs and their brands. Hip-hop and Gen X got to grow up together, sharing the same triumphs and failures in life, music, and money. So many of my memories can be cataloged to a hip-hop soundtrack. That's the power of music—the universal language that speaks to everyone. It can change your mood, it can teach through storytelling, and it can make you move; to take action.

I want to take that same hip-hop story, loop-in iconic records, extend the back stories to the performers, and overlay rhymes that teach money lessons to make you move and take financial action.

– CHILDHOOD –

Music is something that has always spoken to me and made me move. I can remember back as a child, when "Thriller" was the soundtrack and Michael Jackson was a few shades darker. My brothers and I would do our best moonwalking and breakdancing on my parent's linoleum floor with the beats pumping in the background. Those are magic times to look back on when the only thing that concerned us was the music, no adulting needed.

In middle school, I used to shoot hoops listening to such hits like

Arrested Development's "People Everyday" and Kriss Kross' "Jump! Jump!". Remember those young guys wearing their clothes backwards? Great songs to practice to; I loved the beats and hooks. But neither could help my "game", even if I turned my shorts around the wrong way. This 5' 9" country boy was made to be a spectator of sports-which taught me the art of "get in where you fit in". Only a few talented people get to play and far more get to watch them. Just like in music.

Growing up in northeast Ohio, the snow belt-flatlands of Ashtabula, about an hour and a half north of LeBron in Akron, there wasn't much to do, so music and sports became my outlet. Hip-hop was at the intersection of both, but it was completely counterculture to my conservative, rural surroundings. Cleveland was the closest big city, where Browns football trumped a legitimately good CAVS basketball team in the 90's. My dad would play Rush Limbaugh talk radio or country music, and my mother was a fan of early 90's ballads, Enya and Kenny G. Never hip-hop. Our family grew up on 75 forested acres with several crop fields to tend. With three sons, my dad made sure we worked in all seasons, as well as his Vet clinic, and we all made a little chore money every week.

Besides our opposite tastes in music, I am forever grateful we had both a mom and dad who taught us to work hard, save, and modeled an entrepreneurial spirit to us. Many don't get this childhood experience and hip-hop is littered with stories of those who went without and had the streets show them the way instead. Many of those stories with the right hook and beats, found radio time and became hits played across the country, from the dense urban centers to rural farmland. Pre-internet streaming, radio was the medium of musical delivery with records, cassettes, and later CDs, for purchase.

In search of new hip-hop, I would tune into WJMO 92.3 FM (Jammin' 92)—Cleveland's only urban radio station that came through, mostly static-free, on our dual-cassette tape boomboxes. There was a distinct moment that I remember when they announced the new, #1 hot single that would change my life and relationship with hip-hop: "Baby Got Back" by Sir Mix-a-lot. The intro, the beat, the sound effects, and the overt metaphors were entirely different from other music I had ever heard and directly spoke to my early adolescent spirit.

My parents definitely wouldn't approve of this song, but I sure did. Hip-hop, you had my full attention. So, I was moved to take action. On the weekly trek to the mall with Mom, my brothers and I would take some of the chore money we saved to buy new cassette records or singles that I would then play over and over again. That music collection used to be my entire net worth. The simpler times in life, right? I already knew what I wanted to add to my collection that week— and exactly what it looked like. The dead giveaway?

Look for the records with the brand-new parental advisory sticker. This was the government's inadvertent way to make the "good stuff" stand out. There was really only 2 Live Crew, N.W.A., and Public Enemy back then, so the list was almost intentionally short, making those records stand out even more. The thought of walking up and just looking at those tapes made me feel like a rebel—let alone actually buying one and then smuggling it home under my conservative parents' roof!

So naturally, I bought the record with childhood excitement inside and pretended no big deal on the outside. I don't think I felt that way buying something until a few years later when I got a pack of smokes, a lottery ticket, and a Penthouse on my 18th birthday. The conservative stigmas were exciting to break and experience with my first purchases, with my own money. My future financial decisions needed to mature a lot before I started making more sound choices.

Proudly walking back to meet our mother, we got loaded up in the car, seat belts buckled.

She then asked, "What'd you boys buy at the record shop?".

Silence and shrugs.

16

"Drew, what about you?".

I must've looked guilty. "Nothing you'd like to hear".

Mom's instant response, "Oh, well then, let's have a listen".

I took the cassette out to hide the cover art and handed it over. When she popped the cassette in, it was over before it began. The female vocal intro seemed to confuse her, "Oh my god Becky...", but it all became very clear with the opening line:

> **"I like big butts and I cannot lie,**
> **You other brothers can't deny,**
> **That when a girl walks in with an itty bitty waist,**
> **And a round thing in your face, you get sprung! "**

The tape was immediately ejected.

My mom's face looked as if a nuclear reactor was melting down from the "filth" bumping from the speakers. When we were given the freedom of purchasing music with our earned money, if we bought something my parents didn't approve of, there was one major caveat- it would be seized and destroyed. Just like in Monopoly that we played often- you don't pass go or collect $200; it was straight to jail. Tough love ruled our house.

That promise was kept as soon as we got home. By my dad's sledgehammer. A bit too dramatic, but they were making their point. I still asked for my $5 bucks back for the stolen and destroyed merchandise. No dice. Their house, their rules. As the cassette lay there, plastic case in pieces and the tiny black film unraveling from the spools in the breeze, a rebel with a cause was born. I had officially become part of hip-hop culture. What did I learn from this?

Words have weight and hip-hop was dangerous—just like knowledge. Hip-hop was dangerous to this conservative household's upbringing, which intrigued me even more. "How dare I listen to this music" turned into "How can't I listen to this music?" Music became my gateway to that forbidden knowledge outside my country bubble I was born into. Money lesson?

When you buy something, make sure it works more than just the first time. There's nothing more expensive than to keep replacing items. I had to spend another $5 to buy a brand-new single. You're welcome for the royalties, Sir Mix-a-lot. In 8th grade, sports took a back seat when I discovered the one thing I can do well naturally: play the drum set. To my surprise, I was able to hear most music, pick up drumsticks, and lay down beats. I was especially hooked on those rhythms with funky bass lines and clever, catchy lyrics that I tried to phonetically fumble through. I'm no Eminem and glad I stuck to the drums rather than rap. I do owe both my musical and financial journeys to hip-hop; the 4/4 beats in different time signatures were math and the repetition of that math made finance easier for me to learn.

Around that same time, I remember the first two, inescapable hip-hop mega hits: MC Hammer's "U Can't Touch This" and Vanilla Ice's "Ice Ice Baby". With both of their Top 40 domination, it also begged my own personal racial question about hip-hop, "Both black and white people are allowed to rap?" I knew anyone could listen, even if the lyrical scenes depicted were completely foreign to me. But Vanilla Ice was parodied-off with "Hammertime" and those baggy pants left behind for the anti-police, visceral swearing of hardcore rap. N.W.A. and Public Enemy captured the frustrations of urban youth, and with it, both stardom and negative backlash. Which sold even more records and made them even more famous. Dr Dre. set out on his own at Death Row Records bringing in S-n-oo-p D-o-gg and ushering in the new West Coast era of hip-hop. The dead poet's society of 2Pac vs. Biggie had been born and died within years, but left some of the greatest hip-hop records of all-time.

Those were the days. If you don't know, now you know.

Late into high school and the beginning of college, I was watching, talking, listening, and singing all those classic 1990s hits. The over-the-topness of any Puff Daddy music video, like "All About the Benjamins", with larger-than-life jewelry, glitzy lights, the hottest models, and the most sought-after luxury cars, made me feel both jealous of their lifestyle and driven to succeed for myself. If they can do it, then so can I. The American Dream on steroids. In McMansions and Hum-V's we trust.

Oh, how things have changed 25 years on...

The roaring 90s' tech stock market bubble burst in 2000 and didn't go back to par for nearly another 20 years. 9/11 changed our lives forever and ushered in the surveillance state. The Great Financial Crisis of 2008-2009 tested our will and the modern financial system. COVID was a depression. Not financially if you received government-funded hand-outs or were deemed an "essential worker", but mentally. Hip-hop adapted and changed with the rest of us. History gave way to Jay-Z, DMX, and Eminem; then 50 Cent, Kanye West, Drake, and Kendrick Lamar. Don't forget most modern rap is almost all inspired by Lil' Wayne: face tattoos, autotune, indistinguishable lyrics and all. Fortunately, hip-hop has traversed other cultures, bringing about Latin trap and reggaeton stars like Bad Bunny.

Puffy though… is a great reminder to pick wisely who you look up too. Change is the only constant in music, life, and money.

– LESSONS –

From my youth to my middle-aged years, that constant change led both hip-hop and Gen X to cashflow-up and escape debt row together. From our formative years, to having to grow up, get a job, support a family, and plan for our future despite what life throws at us. Hip-hop and I made the same money mistakes together at the same ages- albeit on different sales and scales. In my twenties, I was a broke-joke trying to navigate the money game rules like all those bankrupt rappers. By my thirties, I turned the corner by learning lessons from the school of hard knocks and I got my money right. In my forties? I stand in the shoes of someone who is a successful entrepreneur, like many of those rap moguls we'll discuss in this book.

There's also the reverse diversity of both hip-hop and finance. That same melting pot question we must all answer in society that I felt with MC Hammer and Vanilla Ice. Both industries are dominated by men of different colors. When Vanilla Ice arrived and then was laughed off, it took Eminem, with Dr. Dre's blessing and beats, to re-introduce the hip-hop world to a white rapper. It was an uphill battle to gain credibility and diversity to the culture. As Eminem shamelessly had to own-it on "Without Me":

> **"***I am the worst thing since Elvis Presley,
> to do Black music so selfishly,
> and use it to get myself wealthy.* "**

The finance game is to older, white male financial advisors as the hip-hop game is to younger, black male rappers- and both have a lack of women. Just like everything else, that's changing over time. I can name plenty of rappers who are women, all shades of skin color, and different cultures and languages as hip-hop's global influence has taken hold. Likewise, if you go to the right finance conference hosting the younger demographic of our industry, you'll see that same diversity playing out with money stories that come from good and bad financial choices.

It's about accumulating those zeros and commas; through all the emotions, the mistakes, the triumphs, the downfalls, and celebrations. All that matters is if you're willing to work, learn, and then earn. Do you have what it takes? No labels are needed. Just the willingness.

Whether you're in Gen X, Y, or Z, I'm betting hip-hop has had a profound effect on your learning as well. We watch, we talk, we listen, and we sing. We use our senses to make sense. I bet hip-hop had a profound impact on teaching you financial sense.
It taught me to be proactive and take action. How about you?
Let's take action together.

– WHY? –

Hip-hop has inspired me to move yet again by combining my 20+ year career in personal finance with the soundtrack that taught me the eat-or-be-eaten ways of life. These chapters and words wrote themself, and are as much about hip-hop's story as my own Gen X tale of financial hardships, hard knock lessons, and money-making windfalls. You'll remember the songs and I hope it brings you some nostalgia along the way.

Just like in your own life, you have to learn the money game now more than ever- or deal with the repercussions. Questions like:

"How do I pay-off my school loans?"

"How am I going to buy a house?"

"Will I ever be able to retire?".

These need to be answered; not abandoned for the "YOLO" zeitgeist. Bad money decisions will catch up with you as much as good money decisions will raise you up. Trust me, I'm a CERTIFIED FINANCIAL PLANNER™ sharing my own life experiences throughout this book.

I was, and still am, immersed in my senses—making financial sense fun, not boring. As children, we learn through songs and then it gets lost in textbooks and exams. Why can't we use hip-hop and all the clever wordplay in the rap lyrics to learn the money game? Let's make it light on math, instead using hip-hop superstars' money wins and fails as examples; along with my own "Hard Knock Life" lessons and chapters with intentional titles that drill the point home. I'll bet you'll be able to learn a thing or two, to share and repeat with others.

The Debt Row. Mo' Money, Mo' Problems. Back Yo' Assets Up.

They're titles of tracks in this book, designed to keep you entertained and educated. Equal parts intentional and jesting- to teach through song, clever wordplay, and drive home the most important part of a storyline that you learn as a child in school. Repetition.

The same as how I teach good money decisions to my clients. Repeating the same money rules over and over again as their CERTIFIED FINANCIAL PLANNER™ until they understand it. For instance, saving: "you can't fill a bucket until you plug all the holes".

Just like every great hit hip-hop song has a great beat, it also has a sample and producer. There are rules to every game and finance is no different.

"Can't Touch This"? Credit to Rick James' hit, "Superfreak", and produced by MC Hammer himself.

"Ice Ice Baby"? Credit to Queen and David Bowie's hit, "Under Pressure", sampled by the song's producer, DJ Earthquake for Vanilla Ice.

"Straight Outta Compton" by N.W.A.? Credit to The Winston's and their number one most-sampled song of all-time, "Amen, Brother". Huh? I've never heard of it either, but it's so good it's been used over 6,000 times!

Get your reps in to make muscle memory, but also have a great advisor/producer who knows the money rules/samples. Have a team, do the work, and you'll have a hit financial life too.

Let's have some fun, learn from your favorite hip-hop money mistakes and mine, and get your financial cents corrected so you can throw around some Benjamins of your own. Ready?

Regulators, mount up!

TAKE ACTION!

WHAT WAS YOUR FIRST HIP HOP MEMORY?
HOW DID IT MAKE YOU FEEL?

USE THAT SAME ENERGY TO TAKE ON
YOUR MONEY DECISIONS.

REMEMBER:

1. HIP HOP IS A SAMPLE OF A SAMPLE. YOU DON'T HAVE
TO RE-INVENT THE CIRCLE; JUST USE WHAT WORKS.

2. BUILD A TEAM. JUST LIKE AN ARTIST HAS A PRODUCER, YOU
SHOULD BE WORKING WITH A FINANCIAL PRO.

– END OF TRACK 0 –

TRACK 1.
THE DEBT ROW

TRACK 1: THE DEBT ROW

"*Super Nintendo, Sega Genesis,*
When I was dead broke, man, I couldn't picture this.
50-inch screen, money-green leather sofa,
Got two rides, a limousine with a chauffeur.
Phone bill about two G's flat,
No need to worry, my accountant handles that.
And my whole crew is loungin',
Celebratin' every day, no more public housin'.
Thinkin' back on my one-room shack,
Now my mom pimps a Ac' with minks on her back.
And she loves to show me off of course,
Smiles every time my face is up in The Source.
We used to fuss when the landlord dissed us,
No heat, wonder why Christmas missed us.
Birthdays was the worst days,
Now we sip Champagne when we thirsty.
Uh, damn right, I like the life I live,
'Cause I went from negative to positive."

Just like these iconic lines from Notorious B.I.G's breakout hit "Juicy", hip-hop rhymes are not only nostalgic, but all about boasting and roasting your competitors.

How much money you have, what jewelry you flaunt, what kind of cars you drive, how many women you're surrounded by, but it's almost never about making financial decisions or losing it all. If you make bad money decisions, they will always catch up with you. I know from firsthand experience.

The poetic honesty in this Notorious B.I.G.'s rhyme is unmatched. It's a visual celebration capturing his rags-to-riches lifestyle that lifted himself, his mother, and his entire crew out of poverty. What's missing in his songs are any decisions to invest, rather than blowing his newfound wealth on TV's, cars, limos, minks, and champagne. Perhaps he would've rhymed about investing if he had lived longer.

It takes time, effort, and mistakes to learn the money game and those truths are what real wealth boasts about. Not the shine on your favorite rapper's gold and diamond-encrusted grill or whose face is being tatted up the quickest. We get ahead by making mistakes and learning from them, so let's get busy and learn from the biggest bankruptcy in hip-hop history.

Here's a list of 10 famous rappers who lived their lyrics too long, blew the money they made from their big paydays, and went bankrupt. Which one of them do you think lost $82 million dollars?

Nelly, DMX, Lauryn Hill, Fat Joe, 50 Cent, Ja Rule, MC Hammer, Lil' Kim, Method Man, or Nas?

If you're wondering who "can't touch this" spectacular fall from hip-hop glory, and you guessed MC Hammer; you are correct. Every one of these rappers made big money mistakes, but he landed at the #1 spot.

Way back in 1990, MC Hammer scored the very first hip-hop #1 single with "U Can't Touch This". It was a cultural event that sprung this up-and-coming music niche into the pop music hemisphere, along with his trademark parachute pants and "Hammertime". With massive success though comes massive fame, expectations, and spending. He did not disappoint.

At his peak, he was worth an estimated $70 million. In 1991 alone, he raked in a whopping $31 million, but he spent his fortune faster than he made it. By 1996, he was bankrupt and had a net worth of -$12 million. That's right, he squandered $82 million in the span of a few years. How? He made lots of fatal money decisions.

- He arguably had the largest entourage ever, employing approximately 200 "friends and family" costing him at least $500,000 per month. He later told Oprah it had sometimes been closer to $1 million per month. It takes a village?

- He liked options to get around in style, so he purchased: 17 top-of-the-line sports cars, a private jet, two helicopters, and racehorses… just in case everything else broke down?

- His biggest expense though was his house. It was a 40,000-square-foot mansion which he purchased for a reasonable $12 million. However, he then sunk a further insane sum of money, $30 million, into customizing his casa with classic hip-hop lyrical machismo: statues of himself, the finest Italian marble floors, basketball and tennis courts, and of course: a solid-gold hot tub and toilet.

…and that's how you blow a cool $82 million dollars in hip-hop style. He spent it so fast and furiously that he overspent by $12 million. When the going is good, it takes real family and friends to tell you to slow your roll and perhaps save for a rainy day. Maybe at least not opt for the solid gold hot tub and toilet? Suffice to say, he did not have an accountant or financial advisor.

The silver lining in this story is that MC Hammer eventually turned the corner, learned from his mistakes, and got back to living a wealthy lifestyle by making reasonable choices. That's the school of hard knocks in action. It's expensive tuition, but it's how you get a master's in life.

You may be enrolled there now after "normal" life decisions to go to college, buy a car, get engaged, or get married- no house included. Haven't found the job you need for the cash flow to float your current bills, or pay for the runaway inflation that's skyrocketed prices for everyday items in the last few years? I feel you.

I'm not ashamed to share that I was once enrolled there for years, without hope, after having made terrible financial decisions. Not at all for the hip-hop excesses, but out of necessity to just get by. I survived and thrived after I learned to make good money decisions.

Here's how I fought my way out and practical advice on how you can too.

– WHEN YOU'RE IN A HOLE, STOP DIGGING –

Warren Buffet is generally accepted as the G.O.A.T. of investing, but his famous quote about financial hardship can change your mindset.

"The most important thing to do if you find yourself in a hole is to stop digging."

Simple to say, hard to accomplish. For MC Hammer, it was bankruptcy court and figuring out he couldn't afford to employ a village of people and live like King Louis XVI of France. At least Hammer kept his head? Louis XVI wasn't so lucky.

I have one client who always reminds me of what I ad-libbed when we first spoke about

> **"The most important thing to do if you find yourself in a hole is to stop digging."**
> -Warren Buffett

debt and spending:

"You can't fill a bucket until you plug the holes."

Whatever way it needs to be said to resonate with you, that logic needs to make sense so that thought leads to action.

When we talk about "bad financial decisions", we're referring to the spending and debt that is consuming your livelihood. Everything that's flaunted in a hip-hop video, Keeping up with the Kardashians, and the Instagram-envy consuming our consumption culture. It's not worth participating in. Unplug and be you. You'll feel better and richer.

If you want to get ahead, you must fight back against this normalization of bad debt and spending. This system has been designed to jump from all mediums with ease as time goes by. From 3-minute hip-hop videos glamorizing excess, to the now daily onslaught of 10-second social media clips. They tell compelling lies, confusing mistruths, and prey on your jealousy, to keep you consuming above your means. Social media has only made it more readily available. Don't hate the playa, hate the game.

Hip-hop inspired me to become successful and rich through two of the seven deadly sins: greed and envy. Ever watched a late-1990s Puff Daddy video? He made a mint pretending to have a mint. Most of everything in those videos was rented, but the public, myself included, just assumed it was real life. Any dreams I had before left me wanting more for myself. Because dammit- if he and other rappers could do it, why not me too? The good ol' American Dream bit me in the ass as an adolescent and there was no turning back. What I had to learn is that it's one thing to look rich, and another to actually be wealthy.

Nowadays, you have the same societal-pressured choices I had to make to "Get Rich or Die Tryin", just with updated price tags from inflation and spiked-up interest rates:

- $50,000 for a brand-new car,

- $30,000 for your dream wedding,
- $500,000 for that starter home.

That's not getting rich, that's acting poor. Just in slower ways than those bankrupt hip-hop stars had spent on luxuries and excesses. You can drive a used car for less, you can do a destination wedding for less, and you can save and rent until it's the right time to buy a house, if ever- some people choose not to. Make better financial decisions for yourself and you can become wealthy too.

Speaking about excesses, what about the pressure to run up $100,000 for an undergrad degree? You have to know what your return on investment (ROI) is going to be before enrolling. Forget those entry-level, post-college jobs, will your gold-plated degree increase your lifetime earnings enough to justify that cost? If so, then go for it. If not, it costs less than a pair of Nike sneakers to start a business. In just four years, think how far along you could be compared to your peers who were partying for the same amount of time.

Did you know both Mark Zuckerberg of Facebook and Bill Gates of Microsoft dropped out of Harvard? There's a long list of uber-successful people that dropped out of college to focus on their big idea and enrolled in the School of Hard Knocks to start their entrepreneurship journey.

Get creative, think outside the box, and remember that your parents shouldn't pay your bills. Starting off with hundreds of thousands of societal-pressured debts will put you in a hole for 30+ years. All those quote-on-quote perfect pictures of smiling-happy-people on social media are a lie. Get your priorities right and tune out the noise.

You have to adapt to this trap- stop the madness, drop the bad habits, and roll forward with a plan. Afterall, freedom is the real American Dream, not indentured servitude. Bad debt will imprison you in a hole most won't get out of, even years after trying. It's life on "Debt Row" that you should fear more than buying into the YOLO (You Only Live Once) lifestyle.

Know how I know? Because I made my own near fatal financial decisions that landed me as close to bankruptcy as you can get. Financial "murder was the case they gave me". Here's my "hard knock life" story. An all-too-common one fueled by lack of financial education, terrible money moves, and then how I broke out of the prison I sentenced myself to.

– MY LIFE ON DEBT ROW –

If you don't realize you're in a prison, why would you try to escape? Hip-hop is littered with the same rhymes about people being a product of their surroundings. It's hard to break out of poverty when you are surrounded by it. Lack of education and opportunity are the culprits. It's easier to give up and trade your time for distractions than it is to "Fight the Power" that Chuck D echoed on Public Enemy's hit.

> **"Yet our best trained, best educated, best equipped**
> **Best prepared troops refuse to fight**
> **As a matter of fact, it's safe to say**
> **That they would rather switch than fight."**

If this becomes your sense of community, how do you learn how to break out? You have to wake up to the debt sentence you've been born into. My spin on Notorious B.I.G.'s opening line in "10 Crack Commandments":

"You gotta trust me, I've been in this debt game for years, it made me an animal. There's rules to this game, so here's my manual. This my step-by-step booklet on how I f*cked up, woke up, and broke free by rule number three."

Wake up and step up.

I OWE $100,000 IN BAD DEBT

At my lowest financial point, I woke up one morning with a financial noose around my neck. Not unlike anyone else that's 25 years old now, so I'm preaching to the choir. Just like you, for years it had been accumulating from age 18 at an ever-increasing rate. First, university,

then car, and then basic living expenses to survive.
Here was my bad debt breakdown:

STUDENT LOANS -$25,000
Instead of the average $100,000 in student loan debt nowadays, I only owed $25,000. The interest rate in the early 2000's was around 6-7%, very close to now, but you can see the cost has damn-near quadrupled in 20 years. Ouch.

FAMILY LOANS -$25,000
I owed $25,000 to my parents. To be fair, I had either forgotten about this small detail or chose not to listen, so I was shocked to be handed a congrats card and debt-payback schedule when walking out of my college graduation. Yes, you read that right.

My parents are not like your parents. They're gangsta. They are self-made, middle-class millionaires that graduated from the school of hard knocks themselves. Definitely not a school that ever focused on emotional quotient (EQ) or one that handed out finisher medals where everyone wins. They are old school and in life, there are merely winners and losers. Not that they believed second place was first loser, but if you had a debt, you repaid it. Story over.

The struggle gives you purpose™ and so it was intended for me and my brothers. A totally different moral and ethical conversation, but they had taken out loans against their home equity line with 6% juice (interest) accumulating the entire time I was in school, and it needed to be paid back by me, myself, and I starting two weeks after graduation.

CREDIT CARDS -$50,000
At my worst, I owed over $50,000 in credit cards. Pause game. You're probably wondering what, how, why? Let me tell you my money lie.

What exactly did that buy? Not a new car or anything fun like bottles in da' club. It was spent on things like rent and food to just get by, just for years. When you're a "SEE" (self-employed entrepreneur) and you see you have no income coming in, you have to buckle down and take on debt to smooth out the fat and lean periods. That or you take the "L", tuck your tail, and go back to work at a nine-to-five.

How does a financial advisor helping others get financially right go so wrong? Three words: stubbornness, hopes, and dreams. I wanted to make bank as a successful financial advisor, and I refused to quit until I realized my dream. There was no plan B when I started down this path. Only that this career spoke to me, and you could make a lot of money for your clients and yourself. Starting as a college intern at Merrill Lynch ("The Lynch"), I knew that this world of finance was my future and I could will it into existence—just like my favorite rappers did.

Queue Wu Tang Clan's "C.R.E.A.M." (Cash Rules Everything Around Me):

> "It's been 22 long hard years of still strugglin'
> Survival got me buggin', but I'm alive on arrival
> I peep at the shape of the streets
> And stay awake to the ways of the world 'cause sh*t is deep
> A man with a dream with plans to make C.R.E.A.M"

Youth is naive, and I couldn't have possibly understood the struggle I had signed up for—to build a book of business, to survive in the industry, the amount of money it costs, and the unpaid time commitment to do so.

– ENTER THE 'DEBT' CHAMBER –

After I graduated college, I was greeted by a parental loan I didn't know I had and another that would almost cause financial suicide: Discover Card mailed me a brand-new card with a $20,000 limit. They were very bullish on my future, or more likely, playing the numbers game that my degree would translate to both my financial security and profits for them. I wonder if this is what happens when one gets famous, makes millions of dollars, and gets offered a no-limit card.

For me, the debt department at Discover Card essentially said, "Congratulations! Now take this debt card with a limit more than what you earned in four years of college and make good choices even though you haven't had a financial literacy class". The kicker? I didn't really use it often and when I did, I always paid it off like you're supposed to. That is, until I quit my college job and went for my dream job in finance.

Checks are relics of the past in a digital world, but have you ever had any credit card cash advance checks mailed to you? All you have to do is write in your name, amount, sign, and deposit. The money is in your account the next day. When I had no checks coming in from work, these became my crutch to pay my rent, my food, and my utilities. "Just the essentials", I told myself. Doing that for a couple of years and then having to replace a car on credit and presto, you're in a helluva, deep, dark, hole of bad debt. That was my hard-knock life syllabus. How'd I graduate?

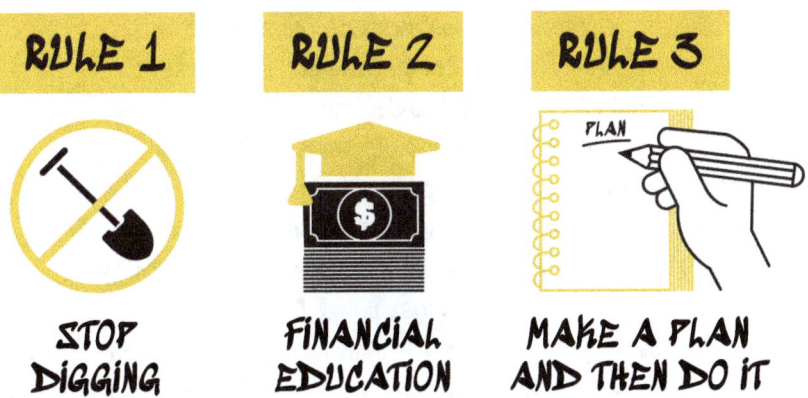

RULE 1	RULE 2	RULE 3
STOP DIGGING	FINANCIAL EDUCATION	MAKE A PLAN AND THEN DO IT

RULE #1: STOP DIGGING.
This had to stop, and it started with me. I made big financial mistakes maxing out my cards and had to stop digging in order to escape.

RULE #2: FINANCIAL EDUCATION
You have to learn from your bad money mistakes in order to become free. No one is coming to save you. WHY?

Being in debt keeps others in control. It's always been this way. Free yourself or become just another worker bee in debt to their knees. It doesn't matter if you grew up in the ghetto or another non-affluent area- you're growing up full of dreams without means. The struggle is normalized, and legal means of escaping aren't emphasized. The quick and easy hip-hop solutions jump out.

As described by Kendrick Lamar in "Money Trees":

"Parked the car then we start rhyming, ya bish,
The only thing we had to free our mind,
Then freeze that verse when we see dollar signs,
You looking like an easy come up, ya bish,
A silver spoon I know you come from, ya bish,
And that's a lifestyle that we never knew,
Go at a reverend for the revenue
It go Halle Berry or hallelujah,
Pick your poison tell me what you do,
Everybody gon' respect the shooter,
But the one in front of the gun lives forever,
And I been hustlin' all day, this a way, that a way
Through canals and alleyways, just to say,
Money trees is the perfect place for shade and that's just how I feel,
A dollar might, just f*ck your main b*tch, that's just how I feel,
A dollar might, say, "F*ck them n****s that you came with",
that's just how I feel,
A dollar might, just make that lane switch, that's just how I feel,
A dollar might, turn to a million and we all rich, that's just how I feel
Dreams of living life like rappers do,
Bump that new E-40 at the school,
You know big ballin' with my homies,
Earl Stevens had us thinking rational,
Back to reality we poor, ya bish,
Another casualty at war, ya bish."

It's all ballin' or dreaming of ballin'. Living in the reality of being poor and with no other legal way out, that's fundamentally wrong and one-sided. You can make it many legal ways, but it starts with money education so you can make less bad financial decisions in life.

Good thing they teach a national curriculum in high school, right? Wrong. There isn't one. Want to know the only time you have to pass a financial literacy course in the US? Answer: bankruptcy court.

Just ask MC Hammer, 50 Cent, and the rest of that list. In order to file Chapter 7, 11, 12, or 13 bankruptcy proceedings, you must complete Credit Counseling. Our US system is so backwards that our government waits for you to fail before they require you to become educated. Which makes sense with a government who spends $1.25 for every $1 they make per year. Every year. Want to smell your computer burning? Go to www.usdebtclock.org.

The current system encourages you to overspend and pretend. I was forced to stop pretending and taught myself how to escape. It shouldn't have to be that way.

RULE #3: MAKE A PLAN.

If the schools aren't teaching good personal finance and our government is modeling bad debt problems, then you need to take the lead in making good money and debt plans. Without one, you become just another person in a prison with no plans to escape. At my lowest, I couldn't stop and wouldn't stop until I got free. In my desperation, I looked for every possible way to reach my money and life goals. That desperation, curiosity, and willingness to make a plan of change had me looking everywhere for the answers.

I found my solution had been hiding in plain sight. Tip: don't try to reinvent the circle when making plans. If you've never made one before, the easiest way is to copy one that worked for someone else- famous or not. That's what I did, and it worked better than I could have hoped for.

EDUCATION FROM DESPERATION AND INSPIRATION.

Sometimes practical financial education comes from surprising people around you. Perhaps it's family, friends, or the teller at the bank. "Work hard and save." "Don't spend more than you make."

The plain vanilla advice works, but it doesn't make the same impression when a celebrity businessman long referenced in hip-hop gives it. That was my "ah ha" moment to listen and gave me the key to becoming debt-free.

Remember Mac Miller's 2011 surprise hit "Donald Trump"? The chorus rhymes:

> **"Take over the world when I'm on my Donald Trump sh*t Look at all this money! Ain't that some sh*t?"**

Trump's brand has always been brash bravado, doing "big" things, and flaunting his wealth and supermodel wives. What's more hip-hop than that? He might as well have released a hip-hop record to go along with all the buildings, books, golf clubs, bibles, and shoes. After his June 2024 New York conviction for business fraud, he's gained even more street cred as a felon. Throw-in surviving an assassination attempt in July of the same year and his "Don't Call it a Comeback" LL Cool J-style Presidential re-election in that November, Trump is, quite frankly, hip-hop's first President.

He's been one of the most enduring symbols of success in hip-hop. So much so that he's been name-dropped in songs from as early as 1991 to the present. A quick sample:

A Tribe Called Quest's 1991 "Skypager":

> **"Beeper's Going Off Like Don Trump gets checks, keep my bases loaded like the New York Mets"**

Wu Tang Clan's Raekwon's 1995 "Incarcerated Scarfaces":

> **"Poisonous sting, which thumps up and acts chumps, Rae's a heavy generator, but yo, guess who's the black Trump?"**

Nelly's 2000 mega-hit "Country Grammar":

"From broke to having brokers, my price is Range Rover.
Now I'm knocking like Jehovah.
Let me in now, let me in now.
Bill Gates, Donald Trump let me in now.
Spend now, I got money to lend my friends now."

Kanye West's 2010 "So Appalled":

"I'm so appalled, Spalding Ball,
Balding Donald Trump taking dollars from y'all.
Baby you're fired, your girlfriend hired,
But if you don't mind, Ima keep you on call."

Say President Trump's name nowadays and it's a lightning rod as much as it's ever been. Back in the early 2000's, like Kanye was referencing in "So Appalled", he had a hit show called The Apprentice where his key line each episode was, "You're fired" with that signature cobra-attacking hand shape spitting venom in the direction of the unlucky contestant's face. Similar to a hip-hop rap battle, but in a boardroom.

Millions were entertained and tuned in each week to see who was kicked to the curb, myself included. I loved the raw, eat-or-be-eaten New York City style. True, gritty, hip-hop attitude. That's how I remember it, so when I was a broke-joke on my come-up, The Apprentice had me at the first "You're fired".

If "The Donald" could tell me how he did it and show me the qualities I needed to hustle and "make it" too, I was all in. Being in debt up to my ears, but still giving my best every day as a financial advisor, I looked up to the raw capitalism in The Apprentice for weekly advice, and the hip-hop songs reinforced it all. I couldn't get enough. It was my great escape for an hour every week. Desperate was the best noun to describe me and the place my mind was living in.

Desperate to make money.

Desperate to pay off my bills.
Desperate to get control of my life.
And lastly, desperate for success.

I had so much to learn, so I started reading two of his books: The Art of the Deal and The Art of the Comeback. Don't give me that eye roll, I know you've done some version of this before for another celebrity in the name of pop culture that you wanted to identify with.

Guess what? He had the help of some great ghostwriters who made the topics both entertaining and educational with, of course, a heavy helping of his businessman narcissism.

Guess what else? I learned how to play for keeps too. "The Donald's" books and Notorious B.I.G. 's rhymes taught me two of the most important things about debt that would help me escape.

DEBT ISN'T A RIGHT, IT'S A PRIVILEGE

Both the lender and borrower need to be kept honest.

Another classic line from Notorious B.I.G.'s epic "10 Crack Commandments":

> *"Number six, that g*ddamn credit? Dead it*
> *You think a crackhead paying you back, sh*t forget it."*

Just like a drug dealer isn't going to extend you "credit" on his merchandise, you can't just walk into a bank and demand a loan for $100 million dollars to buy an apartment complex in Manhattan. You have to earn the privilege and show them you have "the goods" or net worth and cash flow to pay the bank back on time, every month. This of course must be verified by the bank's underwriters aka the bank loan department of "yes" or "no". So, I assume when "The Donald" secured his loans, his brand name and hip-hop persona were taken into account. Knowing what we do now, and from personal experience, real estate investors tend to overstate the value of their properties for loan purposes and understate their values for tax purposes.

If a bank underwrites someone for a bad loan and they belly-up, the bank has to take a charge-off. That's all on them and the primary reason for bank failures. They don't like this very much, so point number two:

BANKS WOULD RATHER GET SOMETHING THAN NOTHING.
Renegotiate your debt.

In his book The Art of the Comeback, "The Donald", found himself going from the title of billionaire to a net worth-lessness of -$1,000,000,000, and back positive again. I had found solace in this because I was only -$100,000 of bad debt. If he could do it, so could I, as long as I copied the same techniques.

I just had to negotiate my bad debt like he had.

STEP 1: Communicate.
STEP 2: Renegotiate.
STEP 3: Move on.

– HOW I PAID-OFF MY BAD DEBTS –

-$50,000 OF CREDIT CARD DEBT
If you're somehow feeling like it's dishonest or morally wrong to call into a bank and threaten non-payment, then I have two soul-cleansing facts for you:

1. It should be illegal for banks to charge 20-30% interest rates on credit cards, and
2. By no coincidence, they have an entire department waiting to speak with you. It's called the "debt remediation department".

Some relevant hip-hop advice about frustration and moving forward in life? Straight from 2pac's "Keep Ya Head up":

"And even though you're fed up

Huh, ya got to keep your head up
keep ya head up, ooh, child, things are gonna get easier
keep-keep ya head up, ooh, child, things'll get brighter. **"**

You can do this all yourself by following Trump's three straightforward steps: communicate, renegotiate, and move on.

STEP 1. COMMUNICATE: "i CAN'T PAY YOU THIS MONTH."

When you call your credit card company and say, "I can't pay you this month", this sets off the alarm bells at the bank. This has changed a bit in the last 15 years, but you'll be transferred to their debt remediation department because banks would rather get something rather than nothing, and not get tied up with collections and bankruptcy proceedings.

STEP 2. RENEGOTIATE: YOUR INTEREST RATE AND PAYMENT TERMS.

When I called in threatening non-payment, I distinctly remember happily accepting the first offer I was presented with from the debt remediation department. "My plan" had worked so well, I thought I had gotten punked.

How well? I went from 29.99% down to a flat 5% rate on a $20,000 maxed-out debt card. The only catch was that I had to agree not to use the card anymore (froze it), pay a flat amount for 60 months ($300 less than what I was paying before), then they'd close-out my account. Lesson learned: banks would rather get something than nothing.

I'll spare you the entire math, but I immediately called each debt card company up and saved not only my credit score, and possible bankruptcy, but freed up nearly $1,000 each month in cash flow, paid-off 40 years earlier, and saved a whopping $125,000 in future interest payments!

STEP 3. MOVE-ON... TO THE NEXT DEBT.

Do you see why I accepted it immediately before they changed their minds? I had found my guaranteed debt-payoff. Talk about putting a spring in your step and a purpose back in life. I felt like a winner with hope for a brighter future once again.

Fast forward to that very last payment. I want that for you too. Is there even a word? Perhaps "joy" or the Pharrell Williams' song "Happy" blasting on 11? For me, that was the feeling.

The feeling of tackling an otherwise insurmountable goal in a shorter amount of time than previously thought will make you absolutely bulletproof in life. What's more hip-hop machismo than that? 50 Cent's surviving nine shots had nothing on me. It's a complete financial game changer when you rewire your brain, plan out your goals, and then take action. All opportunities have to be earned.

-$25,000- FAMILY LOANS RENEGOTIATION

Borrowing yet another line from Notorious B.I.G.'s "10 Crack Commandments":

> "Seven, this rule is so underrated
> keep your family and business completely separated."

Who gives their adult child a college graduation card with a "you owe us" payment schedule starting in two weeks as they're walking out of the ceremony? My parents.

They obviously thought they were doing the right thing by ripping the band-aid off. It doesn't matter what I nor anyone else thinks. I was raised old school by OG's.

After a couple years of learning the finance game and making those monthly payments, there was one Christmas where my brothers and I were handed Christmas cards as "gifts". My parents said they wanted to do something "very special" for us that year. They knew we all needed money, so my immediate thought was, "Yes! Perhaps it's $1,000?". Wrong. You don't get that when you're raised to be accountable with a great accountant. It was a loan forgiveness note for a very odd number like "$3,976". My brothers and I looked strangely at each other at first and muttered "Thanks?". That was an awkward

Christmas. If anyone else out there can relate, please message me. I'll meet you at my next therapy session.

STEP 1: COMMUNICATE: I SAT DOWN WITH MY PARENTS.

Being in finance for a few years and seeing clients' tax returns, I immediately thought, after saying "thanks…", that that specific number of loan forgiveness meant something specific for tax purposes. I waited a few days and then asked if we could sit down together face-to-face. Yes, in fact it was for that tax purpose.

Lesson: this is why you need a good accountant. Sometimes it's not what you make, it's what you save.

Next fact, the majority of my loan was for a truck I used so I could work and provide for myself in college. Knowing what my clients do and that my dad had that same accountant, I asked:

a. Was I deducted off their taxes while I was in school? Yes.
b. Did my dad's accountant depreciate (write-off) my vehicle as a business vehicle? Yes.

Lastly, the mutual fund company where I was working as a financial advisor allowed us and any family members to invest for free. In the mid-2000s it was normal to pay a 5% charge upfront: invest $100, start at $95. In all fairness, they hadn't realized this benefit, so once I laid out their savings plus the positive investment returns for the previous two years, my case had been made.

STEP 2: RENEGOTIATE: HIT THE RESET BUTTON.

My parents forgave the remaining balance and considered it paid in full. I do not know nor care if they wrote off the rest on their taxes—all I cared about was that I was on a roll to clearing my debt load. Facts: My credit cards would be paid-off in five years. I owed my parents $0.

STEP 3: LASTLY, MY STUDENT LOANS.

Now, to use the same tactics on my student loans I did with my debt cards and call Uncle Sam down at the Department of Education.

-$25,000 FEDERAL STUDENT LOAN RENEGOTIATION

Two down, one to go: my Department of Education Federal Student Loans. Spoiler alert: It was over before it began.

I had peak-level, hip-hop, revenge-machismo, like 2pac's classic diss track "Hit Em' Up", when I called in to renegotiate. I had heard of clients' horror stories about attempting this and then hitting a wall or some technicality snag. That's the federal government's jargon for "nice try but isn't going to happen for you." I also knew from my financial advisor courses that federal student loans cannot be discharged in bankruptcy. Back then, I wasn't even sure if you died, they would be canceled.

STEP 1: COMMUNICATE: I CALLED THE D.O.E. AND WAS D.O.A.

The call to the Department of Education didn't go at all as planned. For context, I wasn't trying to apply for loan forgiveness—that didn't even exist in the mid-2000s. I was trying to get the best interest rate and payment to put this debt behind me.

The customer service rep explained what I hadn't realized: my interest rate on my student loan was already the lowest at 6% that I could get and for the longest term available; 20 years.

STEP 2: RENEGOTIATE?

The voice on the other end of the line was straightforward and exact.

"You aren't eligible for a better rate or a longer term".
"Oh. Ok, so I can't…?" I said.
"No." she said. "Game over. This debt was set."

STEP 3: MOVED-ON-DEBT FREE!

For me at 6%, my student loans cost me the most interest, so every time I made extra money, that extra got paid towards the principal (what you actually owe; not interest) and paid it down faster. Doing this, I was able to pay off all my students in seven years, not the original 20! Another milestone in my financial journey that I celebrated.

Believe me, it was a special day to see $0 bad debt. No more debt cards. No more payments to my parents. No more loan payments to Uncle Sam, but you always have to pay your income taxes. I can't wait for you to feel that feeling. When you stop digging, make a plan, and you are set free from the Debt Row.

Cue Ice Cube's, "It Was a Good Day":

> **"**Get me on the court and I'm trouble
> Last week, f*cked around and got a triple double
> Freakin' n****s every way like M.J.
> I can't believe, today was a good day (sh*t) **"**

It can be done. Get to work and start making those calls.

TAKE ACTION!

RULE 1: WHEN IN DEBT, STOP DIGGING.
RULE 2: GET FREE THROUGH FINANCIAL EDUCATION.
RULE 3: MAKE A PLAN AND THEN DO IT.

THE ABC's OF GETTING OUT OF DEBT?

A. COMMUNICATE "I CAN'T PAY..."
B. NEGIOTIATE TO BETTER TERMS,
C. MOVE ON BAD DEBT FREE.

- END OF TRACK 1 -

Track 2.
That G*ddamn Credit, Dead it

TRACK 2: THAT G*DDAMN CREDIT, DEAD IT

"No, I already graduated
And you can live through anything if Magic made it
They say I talk with so much emphasis
Ooh, they so sensitive

Don't ever fix your lips like collagen
And say something when you gon' end up apologin'
Let me know if it's a problem then
Aight man, holla then

La, la, la la (ayy)
Wait 'til I get my money right (yeah)
La, la, la la (yeah)
Then you can't tell me nothing, right?
Excuse me, was you saying something?
Uh-uh, you can't tell me nothing (yeah)"

From Kanye West's "Can't Tell Me Nothing"

Bad credit mistakes can cost you dearly. It certainly did for many clients I've helped steer back to financial clarity, including myself. There are two important sides to credit: one to charge on a card and another to make sure you get the credit. Fortunately, for all of our credit problems, Kanye West will make you feel a whole lot richer on both sides of that coin.

Being one of the few eccentric-megalomaniac-genius-rapper-producers of the 2000s, Kanye enjoyed big hip-hop hits and even bigger public, cringe-worthy faux pas. From saying President George Bush "doesn't care about black people" post-Hurricane Katrina, to interrupting Taylor Swift at the VMAs saying "Imma a let you finish, but Beyoncé had one of the best videos of all time!", his creative genius managed to churn out more hits and then a wildly successful pivot into the fashion arena.

Kanye got to design his first shoes with Adidas back in 2006, but they never got released. Then in 2009, the Yeezy Brand was officially launched with a Nike collaboration on the Nike Air Yeezy.

Why "Yeezy"? It's said to be Kanye's shout-out to his mentor, Jay-Z.

After a five-year collaboration, he ended his partnership with Nike. Why? Simple: he wasn't making any money. Due to contractual minutiae, instead of paying royalties for his designs, Nike opted to donate Kanye's share to a charity of his choice. You have to learn before you earn, son.

Adidas came back calling again in 2015, but this time, approached him for a lucrative, creative partnership. Unlike Nike, they offered to pay royalties for his designs: a whopping 15% wholesale royalty. To break that down, that's before any expenses, or for every $500 shoe sold, Ye banked $75! What followed were star-studded promo releases and his signature footwear selling out in minutes. He had made every entrepreneur's wildest dreams come to life again. First in music, and now as footwear's biggest star.

Unfortunately, his uncontrolled ego led to outrageous rants and demands put on public display. Despite these PR nightmares, Adidas didn't want to stop the printing presses on the $1.8 billion cash influx machine Kanye contributed, in 2022 alone, to their corporate profits. He had single-handedly made the company viable again in typical Kanye style.

Ever been to an underage house party where the music just stops and out pops a parent yelling for you all to go home? Here are Kanye's famous last corporate words on the Drink Champs podcast: "I can say antisemitic things and Adidas can't drop me. Now what?"

Mind you, Adidas is a German company that is acutely aware of the systematic Holocaust murders of six million Jews that took place during WWII in their country. There's a red line and Kanye's ego had leapt across it.

Pride always comes before the fall. Inserting another profound Warren Buffett-ism: "It takes 20 years to build a reputation and five minutes to ruin it. If you think about that, you'll do things differently."

"Now what?" became a simple corporate action for Adidas. Goodbye Kanye and a startling $1.5 billion to his wealth that evaporated overnight. He's made recent headlines this year from his low-fi Super Bowl #58 Yeezy ad and his Vultures 1 and 2 albums have gained praise. Back to Adidas? I think not, but perhaps another struggling brand will. This situation of lost opportunity is best rhymed in Jay-Z's "The Story of O.J." One where his regrets over missed money moves can't help playing him the "DUMBO".

"I coulda bought a place in Dumbo before it was Dumbo
For like 2 million
That same building today is worth 25 million
Guess how I'm feelin'?
Dumbo."

Being that he was Kanye's musical mentor, Jay-Z's lyrics in this song are the perfect bridge from bad money regrets to how double-a-dollar financial knowledge works. Jay-Z has lived the highs and lows of stardom. All angles of the come-up, developing staying power, and a plan for his family to stay in power. Safe to say, he's worked hard on his own finances to go from broke to billionaire status two-and-a-half times over.

Jay-Z then asks the CREDIT question and provides the answer on "The Story of OJ":

> **"You wanna know what's more important than throwin' away money at a strip club? CREDIT. Financial freedom my only hope F*ck livin' rich and dyin' broke"**

Then, how that compounded wisdom played out for him:

> **"I turned that 2 to a 4, 4 to an 8 I turned my life into a nice first week release date Y'all out here still takin' advances, huh? Me and my n****s takin' real chances, uh"**

He's rhyming about his misunderstanding of credit, how he achieved his own financial freedom, and lamenting about other rappers' use of advances- a form of credit, paid upfront to artists and used against them to offset any sales up to the amount. Being a record executive, he knows all about these.

Since your or my best performances are in the shower or car before work, let's dissect Jay-Z's "million dollars worth of game for $9.99". What comes to mind when you say the word CREDIT?

• My credit card accumulates great points.
• School credits are outrageously expensive for this semester.

Credit is used to buy things now for an extra fee, not saving up to be bought outright later. It can sometimes be used on a card, other times through a loan. There is one number that determines whether that fee is larger or smaller. Your Adult GPA; better known as your credit score. We're going to be talking about your score and why credit, after you get your bad debt settled, is the next stop on your financial success journey.

On that same path to making paper stacks is another word that lurks in the financial shadow of the word "credit". It's always sewed up to it and lurking in the background.

The word? Interest or the money owed on borrowed money. This is an equally interesting, multi-defined, finance term.

- This purchase is interest-free for six months.
- The CEO had a controlling interest.
- I have no interest in learning about my credit score.

That last bullet point though- you need to. Burying your head in the sand is for ostriches, and they do it for the distinct purpose of turning their eggs around in their underground nest—not intentionally looking away from their problems.

Be purposeful with building your credit score and you will be rewarded. If you don't watch it, pay your bills late, and/or are careless with your finances, you won't find anyone to cry to when you pay the absolute highest costs (i.e. interest, penalties) for loans.

That is, if you can even get loans. There's a reason why rappers are given advances, and predatory PayDay Loans exist: for financially uneducated people that don't have credit nor bank accounts. If you don't want to have to pay your label back for an over-promised advance from under-delivering sales or a 400% PayDay loan, you should keep reading. Let's keep your interest in credit primed with another big-baller number.

– $170,000,000 –

Just as ridiculous as Kanye's antics, record label predatory advances, and paying 400% in interest for PayDay loans, there are obscene purchases made on credit.

How big? The largest purchase ever made on a credit card was a cool $170 million. That's right- nine digits, seven zeros, and two commas: $170,000,000. In one auction. For one painting. By an artist with a name that has as many syllables as "neuropharmacologically."

I challenge anyone to spit that or "Amedeo Modigliani" at your next rap battle. You'll leave your opponent and crowd just as confused as the story behind this mind-blowing purchase.

Back in 2015, the same year that Yeezy brand launched, a former Shanghai-taxi-driver-turned-Chinese-billionaire, Mr. Li Yiquia (for ease, we can just call him "Mr. LY") made headlines for placing the winning auction bid of $170.4 million for said Amedeo Modigliani's risqué "Nu Couché" (or in English, "Reclining Nude") on his no-limit American Express Centurion Card.

If you're staring at the nude model in this piece of art, you might be wondering the same question I am, "Why is the pillow blue?" For real though, "Why would a billionaire use a credit card to buy a painting when they can just pay with their mountain of cash?"

Remember Jay-Z's lyrics about credit and financial freedom? Billionaires, like other successful people, have multiple sources of income, assets, savings, and yes- even debt, just on a much larger scale of zeros and commas.

[1]If your net worth (what you own – what you owe) is tied up in real estate, stocks, and art (just like Jay's) you can become cash-strapped: not being able to access enough money for your impulse purchases. Enter the world of purchasing-ease using credit. Where your net worth, credit score, and interest add up bigger than the Empire State.

[1]*Stock investing includes risks, including fluctuating prices and loss of principal.*

Modern case-in-point: one of the world's richest men in the world, Elon Musk, has his net worth primarily held in stock of the companies he's either started and taken public, like Tesla, or privately-owned, like Space X. His salary is intentionally $0 for tax purposes. How does he pay for anything? When he needs money, he just takes loans out against his stocks, which are not taxed, with VIP low-interest payments, and then pays it back by selling the least amount of stock possible. This helps Mr. Musk and other billionaires using this same tax strategy to pay the very least in taxes.

– REMEMBER LOANS = CREDIT; BORROWED MONEY THAT COSTS YOU HONEY –

This is all part of the legal financial game that you need to understand and apply to your life and your finances. At least until you can hire a team that the rich have to keep more of their dough in their bakery and not Uncle Sam's.

Back to that record-setting $170.4 million credit card purchase of Mr. LY. Why did he use his credit card? Because he could.

What use is a no-limit AmEx card if you don't buy ridiculous things that us little people cannot afford, right? He also had a prior credit history of paying off his credit card bill for Billionaire-baller purchases. Just a year before, he paid a then record $36 million for an ancient Chinese porcelain cup and another $45 million for a 600-year-old silk wall hanging. That was his heads up to AmEx that he was going to push his no-limit credit card.

Mr. LY is a man who loves his art, collectibles, and collecting millions of credit card points. Presumably though for these purchases, even billionaires would have had to call ahead to make American Express aware of his plans to get into the Guiness Book of World Records and to keep the points or get a statement credit.

I'm using this No Limit-Cash Money extravagant example to grab your attention and explain my seven rules of how credit works, so you don't end up on Debt Row.

RULE 1: It's the bank's money. Always remember this first rule about credit: it's the bank's money. If credit is mismanaged or fraudulently stolen, they're out a whole lot of paper stacks. They guard this risk appropriately by examining the risk you present them if they loan money to you. How?

RULE 2: Credit is based off your credit score. It's easy to understand: the higher your score, the lower the interest rate. Be responsible, keep your score high, and pay less when you need to use the monetary tool known as credit. Just like our examples of Mr. Musk or Mr. LY, this can be one of your biggest assets to reach your financial goals. Having the ability to purchase or acquire something of value at a given moment is the difference between the would-haves, could-haves, and the should-haves in life. As we referenced Jay-Z before: don't be a "DUMBO".

RULE 3: Credit is another word for loans. As in, if your credit score is high enough, the bank will loan you their money for what you want to buy. For example: home mortgages, student loans, auto loans, personal loans, and credit cards. [2] These are all examples of consumer loans, our focus here, but there are also loans for businesses and governments (aka government bonds).

If you're a billionaire-baller like Jay-Z is and Kanye was, you can get loans against your non-cash assets (aka art, stocks, real estate, etc.), so that you purchase things on demand.

RULE 4: Loans are never free. To piggyback off rule number three, loans are never free. You have to pay interest. Interest is the money the bank gets paid while they wait for you to pay them back in full. If you miss a payment, there are other fees and penalties that can be triggered.

[2] Government bonds are guaranteed by the US government as to the timely payment of principal and interest and, if held to maturity, offer a fixed rate of return and fixed principal value.

You need to take an interest in not paying interest. How much interest do you pay on a 30% credit card if you pay it off each month? Zero, nada. Don't pay the fees, keep your honey away from the bank's bees.

RULE 5: Credit is issued for fixed amounts. Credit and loans for normal, non-billionaire types like you and I, have a pre-set limit that we can charge or be approved for. If you ever get the urge to call up Jacob the Jeweler and get your own Rick Ross-inspired yellow-diamond face chain for a cool $1.5 million, you better call ahead to get your limit approved first.

RULE 6: Credit must be paid back. Either in a set period for a fixed loan or a rolling period for a variable loan. You need to know the difference to get a sense of where your hard-earned dollars are being spent. Fixed loan. A fixed loan is credit issued by secured debt or things that can be taken back from you. Think: home mortgage loan, auto loans, and student loans. You can pay on a house for 30 years, 10-20 years for student loans, and five-plus years for a car. Student loans are considered "secured" because the Feds can collect payment from either your income or assets. These interest rates are by far the lowest, so they cost you the least.

SET PERIOD = FIXED LOAN

A variable loan is credit issued that is unsecure or nothing of value to be taken back from you. Think: Credit cards, personal loans, and buy now/pay later schemes. There is no set length of time, only minimum payments due monthly.

Danger! These interest rates are by far the highest, so you always want to pay these off on time for peace of mind. Again, don't be a "DUMBO" like I was and get put on debt row.

ROLLING PERIOD = VARIABLE LOANS

RULE 7: Credit is a money tool. If you forget rule number six, you're going to be taking some hits to your credit score. Remember, credit is a money tool for purchasing things with the bank's money. The credit the bank may issue you is a privilege, not a right, so it must be paid back in full and with interest. Every month or else "you'll find yourself in some serious sh*t."

The only way to not pay is through bankruptcy. That will Swiss cheese up both your credit score and your ability to borrow by blackballing you from any credit, from any bank, for at least seven years to 10 years depending on the type of bankruptcy.

The silver lining? In order to file bankruptcy, you'll also get to take the required financial literacy test, so you learn how to use credit going forward. I'm sincerely hoping you've decided to read this book instead.

- BANKRUPTCY = WHEN YOU LOSE IT ALL. IS IT FOR YOU? -

Want to put two middle fingers in the air like you just don't care? Better textbook up on bankruptcy proceedings before financial "murder was the case they gave you".

Chapter 7 Bankruptcy: you don't go to heaven. In fact, it's financial hell. Also known as liquidation bankruptcy, Chapter 7 makes you sell off some of your "assets" to settle any secured loans. It's the most common form of consumer bankruptcy and is usually completed within three-to-six months. Those who file for Chapter 7 will no longer be required to pay back any unsecured debt like personal loans, credit cards and/or medical expenses, but you will be required to stay on the consumer's credit reports for 10 years from their filing date. That's right, it'll cost you everything plus a decade of your life. Your G*ddamn Credit? The banks will dead it.

Again, for the people in the back: you'll still owe 100% of your federal student loans. Why? The government always gets theirs.
Chapter 13 Bankruptcy: Not as mean because you still pay some green. This can be referred to as payroll bankruptcy. This form of filing offers a payment plan for those who have the income to repay their debts,

just not necessarily on time. Only about a third of bankruptcies are filed as Chapter 13. Those who file are still required to pay back their debts, but instead over a three-to-five year time frame. Chapter 13 bankruptcies stay on consumers' credit reports for seven years from their filing date. The financial scars show less on this filing, but even after you pay back all your debts, your credit won't forget it for a few years after.

- WHAT'S YOUR ADULT GPA? -

We covered a lot about how not to get your "credit, dead it"- so let's drop the mic on this chapter covering your "Adult GPA". What's a good score, who's responsible for the scoring, and helpful tips and tricks to help you raise the roof on your credit to 800.

Every Gen X'er like me, grew up in an era when schools mailed our grades directly home. I usually tried my best to intercept anything coming home from the school, but Mom and Dad always knew what we were trying to pull. My brothers and I kept them on their toes which is why they had to run a tight ship.

Back then, our grade scale was simply an A through F. I was formally introduced to the GPA-number equivalent in high school and then college. I was a solid 3.0 student balancing school, a part-time job, and a social life, so my studying filled in the gaps. Take it from this author, grades matter, but it's who you know and how hard you work that really adds to your personal game and gain. As my dad has joked:

"What do you call a doctor finishing last in his class? Doctor."

SO, WHAT'S AN ADULT GPA?

Just because you graduate formal schooling, the exams can't stop, won't stop. You're going to get endless "tests" as an adult. One of these is a unique number assigned to you by a company called Fair, Isaac and Company, or FICO. Their FICO score is unlike any other test you've taken before because at first glance there is no teacher or student in a classroom, but you couldn't be more misled.

FICO is the teacher administering the test, the test you're taking is for credit, and your score determines just how good you are at making financial decisions. The big difference is that this test isn't scored and reported per semester, it's reported monthly. It rarely stays the same and it's something to always keep an eye on. Why? Because it tells banks what interest rate you should pay for your purchases on credit. House, car, credit cards, etc. It's all built directly off of your score.

How should you read this number? The higher the number, the lower the interest, which costs you less in interest. The lower the number, the higher the interest, which costs you more in interest. Got it? If you haven't before, stop reading and go check your FICO score now. How? Go to: www.freecreditreport.com.

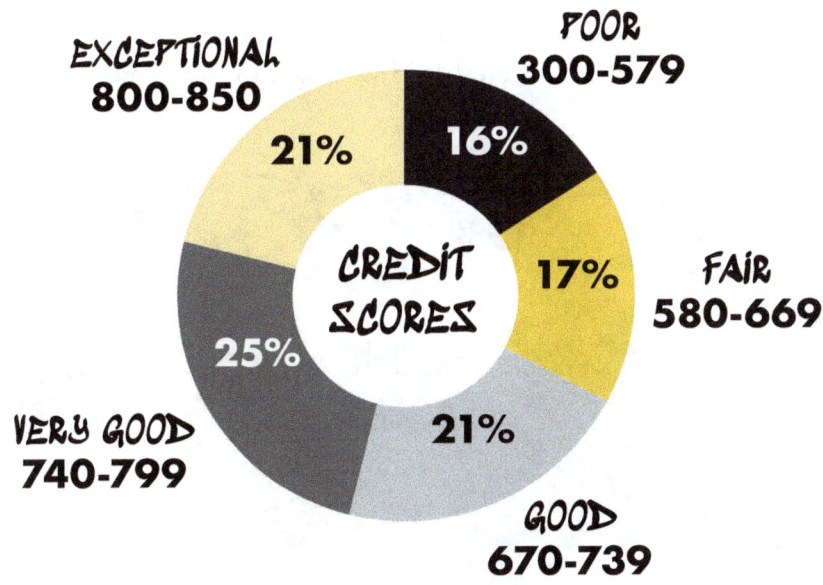

Get in the habit of checking it monthly for any changes or possible fraud. It's one more thing to do to keep secure in this digital world, but that's also why you should update your passwords often. Make it a habit. Now that you know your number, how do you stack up?

The chart right shows credit scores percentages on where most Americans fall into.

Most Americans get to "good" or better. But, if you find yourself in "fair" or "poor", you're going to have to put in monthly work to open that door to be charged less interest—not more. The 411: your goal here is not for an "exceptional" 800+ score, it's only getting to a "very good" score of 740. Why? Because you don't get any better credit rates above 740. How are you going to get there? You need to understand first how your credit score is calculated. Cue the scorecard, tips, and the tricks you need to level up.

TOP 2 CREDIT SCORE FACTORS

35% = Payment History. Have you been paying on time?
30% = Amounts Owed (fix chart!) How much in total have you borrowed?

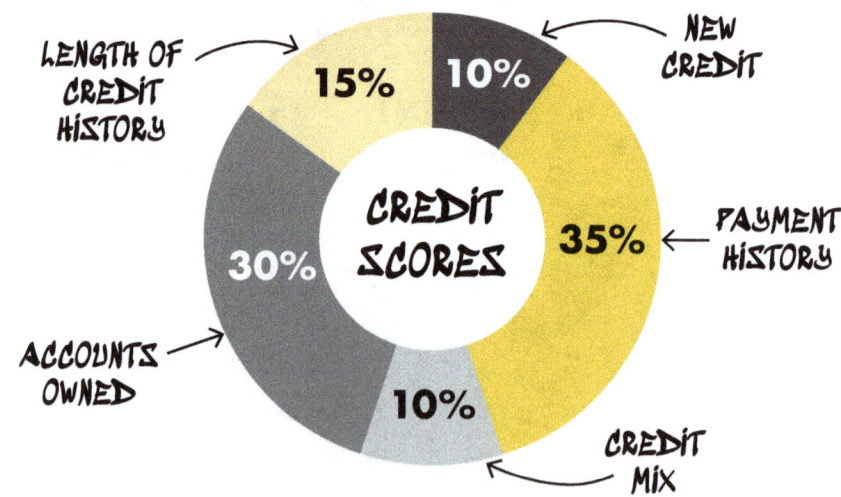

BOTTOM 3?

15% = Length of Credit.
10% = Credit Mix. What types of credit? Home Mortgage, Auto Loan, Student Loans, and/or credit cards.
10% = New Credit. Are you signing up for new accounts?

#1 PREACH THIS RHYME, ALWAYS PAY ON TIME. *Automate your payments with auto-bill-pay. You can't miss a payment and have your score hurt if it's always paid on time. Easy one.*

#2 UNLOAD THE DEBT-WEIGHT MONTHLY. *Do not carry a balance on credit cards—carry points. Your interest rate is always 0% if your cards are paid off, not the 30% the banks want to charge you. Stick to Tip #1 and it can be set up to take care of #2.*

#3 THINK TWICE BEFORE YOU ROLL THE CREDIT DICE. *Do not sign up for every credit offer unless it's able to add value to your mix of credit. That's value-able. Think: different types of credit for different purchases. Also, always keep your oldest accounts open for the length of credit history.*

#4 KIDS NEED SHOES, THE RIGHT ATTITUDES, AND CREDIT HISTORY PURSUED. *If you are a responsible borrower and have a rockstar credit score, then consider adding your little ones as 'Authorized Users' to your credit card accounts. No, they don't even have to get a card, but they will get the automatic benefit at age 18 of a decade-plus of superb credit history. That makes getting approved for loans that much easier. What a gift!*

#5 NEVER DEBIT, ALWAYS DEBT-IT WITH YOUR CREDIT. *There's a big difference between a credit card and a debit card. Credit is the bank's money and debit is your money. If your debit card is hacked, your money can go to $0, and it can take a long time to recover the stolen funds. On the other hand, if your credit card is hacked, the maximum loss is $50.*

Most important point: you don't need to be an A-student to have A-credit (740+), just good ol' fashion adulting 101 responsibilities. You know you got this.

– END OF TRACK 2 –

track 3.

i'm a business, man

TRACK 3: I'M A BUSINESS, MAN

"I'm not a businessman. I'm a business, man."

-Jay-Z on Kanye West's "Diamonds from Sierra Leone"

G*ddamn right he is.

When you're worth an estimated $2.5 billion, you are a business and a highly lucrative one at that. How'd he do it? For that matter, how'd every rapper, myself, or any other small business owner make it?

One word: entrepreneur and the Wu-Tang mindset:

"Cash rules everything around me.
"C.R.E.A.M.",
Get the money,
Dollar, dollar bill y'all!"

Before we analyze the business hustling's of the most successful rapper of all time, let's lay out some basic definitions on how you can make money in the first place. Then you can understand more about an entrepreneur, like Jay-Z. When you boil it down, there are only four ways to make money:

1. Employed: You work for someone who pays you money.
2. Investor: Your money makes you money.
3. Real Estate: You buy property that makes you money, or
4. Self-employed: You work for yourself.

EMPLOYED

If you're at number one: Thank you. You need to learn before you earn, so working under someone else can give you a steady paycheck and experience. This also works out well for those that don't want the pressures of being a boss like Rick Ross. If it were easy, everyone would be doing it. Instead, you trade your time for steady pay, two weeks of vacation, and health insurance. No shame in your game if you want to be in control of your weeknights/ends and have less stress.

INVESTOR

If you have any savings and investments, then you can check-off number two as well. If you have that steady paycheck, you should be stacking cash away for a rainy day and saving for your future through investments. The experienced investor understands the compounded mix of money and time to make your investments grow. Like planting a "money" tree. Invest wisely and to your comfort, and your money will make money for you while you sleep. Albert Einstein once said, "Compound interest is the eighth wonder of the world". Jay-Z gets it, and you need to as well. Keep reading.

> "Compound interest is the eighth wonder of the world"
> -Albert Einstein

REAL ESTATE

When someone buys a home, they are introduced to the world of real estate. To buy that property, the bank wants you to put down somewhere around 10-20% of the purchase price with your cash. The remaining balance is then paid by you by monthly mortgage payments over the next 15 or 30 years.

This is called leverage: using some of your money, but mostly borrowed, to buy an asset of much more value in hopes it goes up more than it cost you.

Real estate investors who buy homes, apartments, and/or office buildings know how to leverage their own cash and cash flow to continue adding more real estate to their portfolio. Why? Real estate can create passive income, preferable tax situations, and also appreciate in value. Confused?

What if you buy an apartment for the fixed price of $500,000, with only 10% down ($50,000). The monthly cash flow (rent) pays for the mortgage (payment to bank), all the while the property's value appreciates to $1,000,000 over time? You 10x'ed your $50K. I'd take that trade all day. This is how 2pac could have legally made "a dollar out of 15 cents".

ENTREPRENEUR

According to Investopedia, an entrepreneur is an individual who creates a new business, bearing most of the risks and enjoying most of the rewards. Entrepreneurs who prove to be successful in taking on the risks of a startup are rewarded with profits, fame, and continued growth opportunities. Those who fail suffer losses and become less prevalent in the markets.

Just like alchemists and magicians, successful entrepreneurs have to make something from nothing. This is the journey ahead for any entrepreneur. Your mere survival depends on whether you can build something from nothing for no pay, no vacation, and in as little time as possible. The only checks you cash are made out to "Hustle Harder." When I was struggling to make something from nothing, my daily diet consisted of two Wendy's 99-cent Junior Bacon Cheeseburgers for lunch. There were no vacations planned. My only focus was how I'd find my next client or be able to pay rent that month. My hopes, my dreams, and the promises I made to myself got me through those uncertain times of self-doubt. Should I just give up or keep going?

No one is ever guaranteed more time or money when they head down their own entrepreneurial path. Some people do use creative ways to motivate themselves- not just the memories of hard times.

At the start of his entrepreneurship journey, 23-year-old comedian Jim Carrey embarked on his now-famous Hollywood career by writing himself a check for $1 million for "acting services rendered". The check's date? 10 years later. He carried it in his wallet on set at *In Living Colour* from 1990 to 1994 until his big on-screen breakthrough in *Ace Ventura: Pet Detective*. He's now worth close to $200 million and reminds everyone, "I wish everyone could get rich and famous and everything they dreamed of so they can see that's not the answer."

That's a humble lesson to take, and one to make sure you know, from the beginning, what your non-financial priorities are. Keep that in focus.

On your journey to become a successful entrepreneur, you'll need a constant reminder of why you're doing what you're doing long after your initial passion begins to wane. For me, it wasn't a $1 million check to myself or to get rich. I only wanted to create a career that challenged me, let me help others, and could provide for a family, a house, vacations, and retire someday. The everyday wants of living in the first world.

In Eminem's *8 Mile*, he shines in an autobiographical tale of his life growing up in the urban trailer parks and ghettos of Detroit. He just wanted out—and rapping was his ticket. He fought against working a dead-end factory job, his stage fright, the stigma of being a white rapper, and the constant doubt of everyone around him, especially his own mother. It was only his inner circle that believed in him long before he ever succeeded.

He failed a lot. He failed before and after getting famous. Failure is something you must become comfortable with, learn from, and overcome. That's Entrepreneurship 101. When you fall, you have to get back up again or risk missing your big break.

Just like the hook in "Lose Yourself":

> **"You better lose yourself in the music**
> **The moment, you own it, you better never let it go (Go)**
> **You only get one shot, do not miss your chance to blow**
> **This opportunity comes once in a lifetime, yo."**

All entrepreneurs fail. Beyond normal fear and self-doubt, they fail to manage their cash flows, or their time, or fail to adapt fast enough to their customers' needs and their business goes under. Most fail more than Michael Jordan's 12,345 missed shots, but the secret is learning from those mistakes, putting in the work, and showing up again and again.

You have to pay the tuition to the School of Hard Knocks through life experience. Only a select few graduates from this elite school experienced the level of money, power, and fame that Jay-Z, Jim Carrey, and Eminem found. Most, myself included, achieve all they need by defining their own version of success by building their own business and career. I know I have, and I don't forget the struggle that it took to sit right here, right now.

It's ironic that Jay's first iconic hit was 1998's "Hard Knock Life". He ingeniously spun the tuition he paid to the school of that same name into a hip-hop anthem everyone could relate to. Entrepreneurship 101: find a niche and then fill it. Turns out the struggle both he and Annie experienced was an emotional niche to fill for millions of people. Especially when you can artfully put a beat and flow to a recognizable sample in four minutes or less.

– ENTREPRENEUR –

Before co-founding his own record label, Roc-a-fella, Jay-Z did what many other rising hip-hop artists had to do without any major label support: he sold his burned CDs out of the back of his car. Every day you have to hustle when you get started. It's the proverbial snowball-to-avalanche momentum that one must successfully harness. It's all the work you have to put in upfront, that no one sees for years before you're an overnight success. The struggle gives you purpose™ and finding your purpose is more rewarding than any returns you can ever dream up.

Co-founding your own record company before creating any hit music shows hustle. He didn't wait to be signed to a major label- he made it happen by believing in his abilities and knowing the rest of the pieces would fall in place. Failure didn't hold him back.

When his talent had the opportunity to shine through on his first hit songs and touring in front of millions, those record sales and revenue from performing live went back to him and his partners who believed in the dream. They took the risks and received the rewards of money, power, and fame.

In true entrepreneurial vision, purposefully building on top of those rising rewards, he took the leap of faith to venture out into different businesses. They were all unique to him, while remaining loyal to his hip-hop brand for his fans.

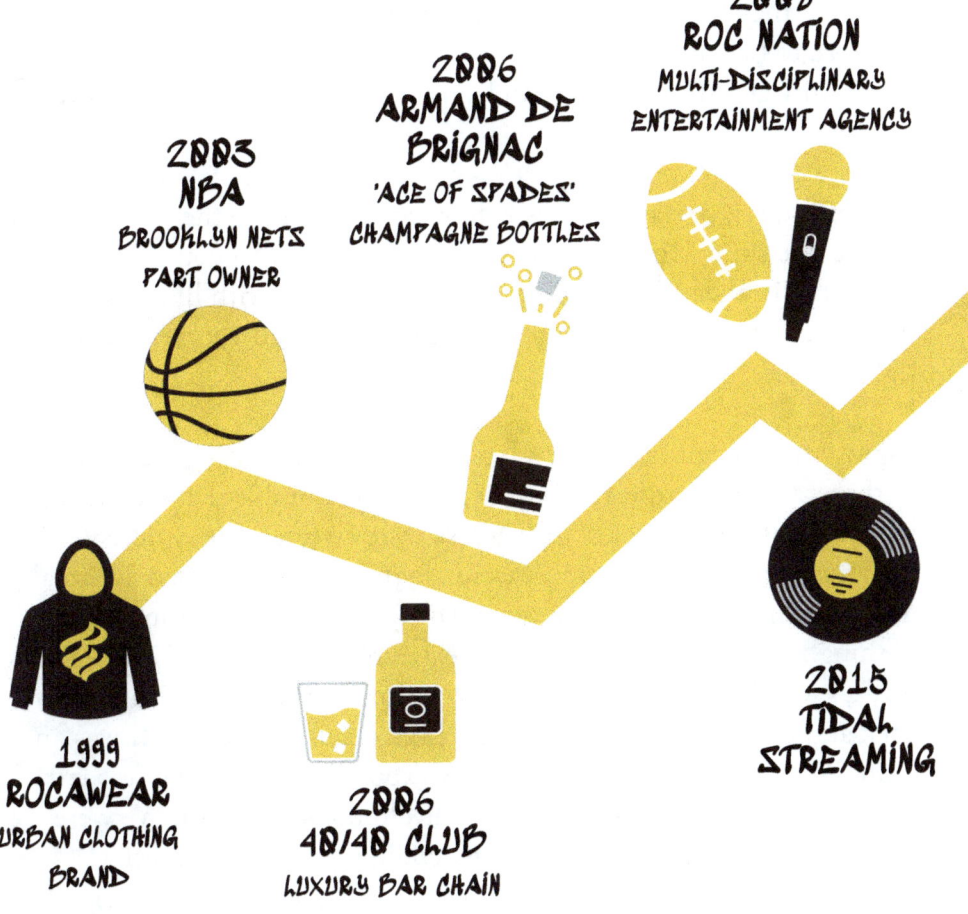

2008
ROC NATION
MULTI-DISCIPLINARY
ENTERTAINMENT AGENCY

2006
ARMAND DE
BRIGNAC
'ACE OF SPADES'
CHAMPAGNE BOTTLES

2003
NBA
BROOKLYN NETS
PART OWNER

1999
ROCAWEAR
URBAN CLOTHING
BRAND

2006
40/40 CLUB
LUXURY BAR CHAIN

2015
TIDAL
STREAMING

All the while Jay-Z was reinvesting into other companies, real estate, art, and perhaps the most important of all: people.

He cultivated a network of friends and rap foes, signed future billionaires like Kanye West and Rihanna to his record labels, and cultivated business and entertainment connections.

In the middle of his entrepreneurial journey towards money, power, and fame, he found the crown jewel in any successful entrepreneur's life: the right partner to support him in life and business. Beyonce, the Queen Bee for billionaire-in-the-making, proved the right collaboration in music ("03 Bonnie and Clyde") and life when they married in 2008.

Together they became bigger than either one could have by themselves and rose to become the entertainment business's most powerful couple. It not only elevated Jay, his brand, and his businesses, but hers as well. 1 + 1 = 3.

One of life's important lessons is this: when you have the right partner and people supporting you, the sky's the limit. When you don't? Struggles lie ahead. This wisdom must be learned with life experience. Wisdom to make the right choices and to surround yourself with the right people.

In my entrepreneurial journey, I eventually started eating steak instead of those 99-cent burgers. I'll never forget my humble daily regimen, because that's what makes my success taste sweeter. Every decision I made through thick and thin was made to survive, and then eventually thrive. Fighting through five years' worth of creating a business from nothing to something. Then the Great Financial Crisis of 2008-2009 (GFC) wrecked the world economy, and my business with it. Just go back and listen to any hip-hop song from that time period. It was an economic virus where everything was exposed, and nothing was left unscathed. People's jobs, homes, and livelihoods were lost. We were peering into the abyss and not many could see a path forward. Jay-Z felt it in 2009's "Run this Town" with Kanye and Rihanna:

> **❝** *But for now let me get back to this paper,*
> *I'm a couple bands down and I'm tryin to get back,*

I gave the other grip, I lost a fifth of five stacks,
Yeah, I'm talking five commas, six zeros, dot zero."

Sounds like he lost a cool $5 million. Pretty sure he made that all back and then some. I may not have lost my job at the time because I was self-employed, but I had to do what all entrepreneurs must do from time to time: completely re-tool my business. I had to be open to new partnerships that would allow my business to survive through the post-GFC world. The silver lining for all crises is that people craving routine and comfort are forced into action and innovation. My action was to say goodbye to costly commissions and innovate to a smaller, yet recurring fee business: very similar to the subscription model in music streaming now that took the place of expensive, standalone records. Like a forest fire that burnt down everything in sight, green sprouts started to emerge from the creative destruction and life moved on.

As my business pivot played out and the economy slowly recovered, so did I. In time, those rent payments I could barely afford turned into a reasonable mortgage for a family home. I graduated from doing free pizza lunch n' learns for prospects to real clients who found my advice worth the price. Each time I signed a new client and made forward progress, I reinvested it back into expanding my business and becoming a better version of myself. Be that through furthering my talent with daily learning, being open to expanding on my initial goals, and strengthening myself and my business' bottom line by being able to save, invest, and pay down my bad debt.

These are the events that forged my wisdom, and what I relied on for the biggest success in my entrepreneurial and life journey: finding my wife.

I'm sure like most successful couples who meet, (even Jay-Z and Beyonce) it wasn't only by chance, or mutual friends introducing them, but it was by listening to their own instincts. From creating a viable business to surviving the GFC, I had become so exhausted listening to all the "no's," that my gut instinct was to have a year of saying "yes" to my personal life.

So, that's exactly what I did in 2010. I said "yes" to every invite, every event, and every trip. Guess what?

I met my Berlin-er wife, I traveled the world making new friends, visiting future family and started thinking more and more about the future I had dreamed of. I was on a bigger and better life path; one I couldn't have imagined before meeting my wife. That's when you know you have found the ying to your yang, or the right to your left hand. It just works better.

Take inventory and ask yourself: who are you surrounding yourself with? Are you gaining wisdom and listening to your instincts? In the 1992 classic, "Don't Sweat the Technique" Eric B. and Rakim, rap about the process and time it takes to cultivate the fruits of your labors. Everything great, takes time, so don't be in a rush until it feels right.

No settling. No diggity.

The partner you choose in life should make you better, dream bigger, and provide support and honest advice. That's surrounding yourself with the right people and then sharing the success. If you look at my life, or Jay-Z's, our choice of spouses made us better than before and multiplied into families. We both had individual business successes before our spouses, but creating a family with your spouse is such a sacred and life-fulfilling act. One you should celebrate and invest your time into above all else. Take my favorite unknown entrepreneur:

– JESSE ITZLER –

Ever heard of him? I didn't think so. He's a former 1980s white rapper, turned serial-entrepreneur, best-selling author, ultra marathoner, and NBA Owner. Jesse Itzler has accomplished more than most people could in four lifetimes. He's also married to Sara Blakely, the billionaire founder of Spanx, and has a beautiful family of six. If you follow him on any social media, he not only celebrates his family above all their business interests and pursuits but maximizes his time to prioritize his family. He does a fantastic job at squeezing out 25 hours-a-day, eight days a week, and as all the hyphens suggest, one hell of an entrepreneurial chameleon.

The first time I heard Jesse speak, I had no idea who he was, other than being billed as a "dynamic entrepreneur" at my work conference. He never once mentioned his wife, Sara, or said "Spanx". But I bet you know most of this hit list:

Jesse grew up in a Jewish family in Roslyn, New York (on Long Island). He graduated from American college and got signed as a white rapper, writing on "Wild Thing" by Tone Loc. He also produced such off-mainstream hits like "College Girls (Are Easy)" and "Shake it Like

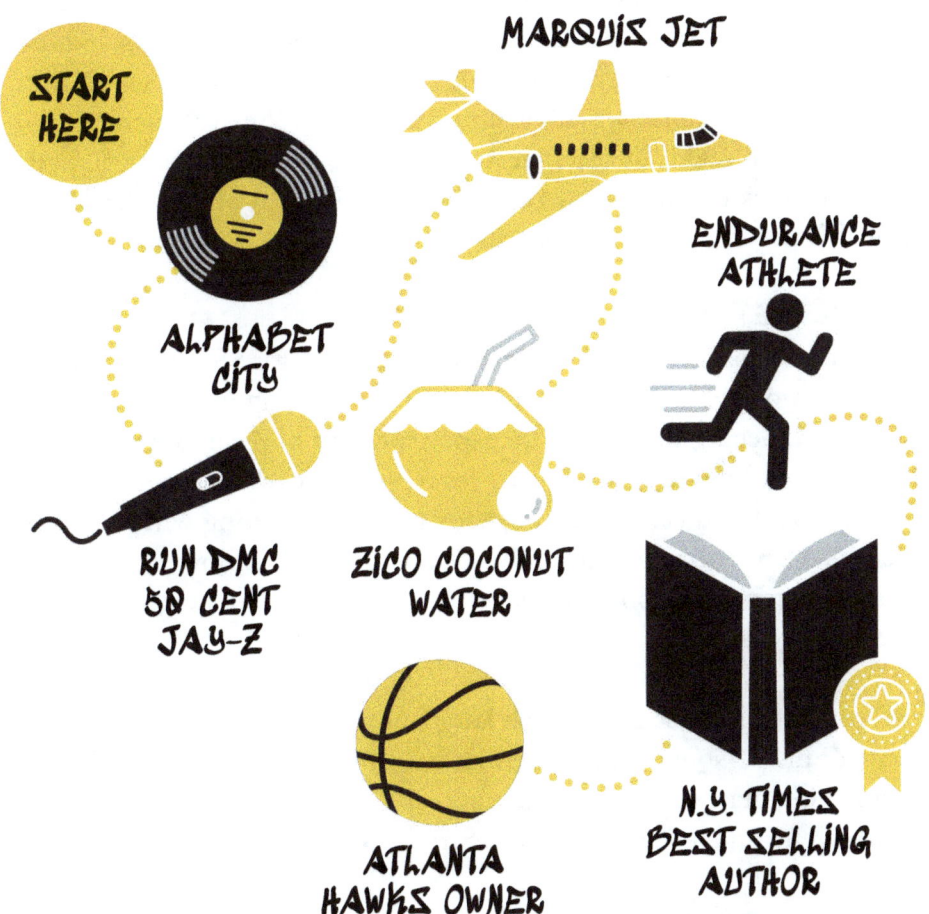

START HERE

ALPHABET CITY

MARQUIS JET

ENDURANCE ATHLETE

RUN DMC
50 CENT
JAY-Z

ZICO COCONUT WATER

ATLANTA HAWKS OWNER

N.Y. TIMES BEST SELLING AUTHOR

a White Girl" but found his musical calling writing for the New York Knicks. Penning their theme song "Go NY Go" and then producing hype-jingles for more than 50 other sports team. You have to find your niche as an entrepreneur, remember? Jesse was on his entrepreneurial way.

ALPHABET CITY

During this time, his company, Alphabet City, managed the iconic hip-hop group, Run DMC. At his office, he shared the same desk with the group's DJ: Jam Master J. One day, a young boxer with hip-hop ambitions shows up and then spends 18 months as his intern to gain experience in the business—it was none other than Mr. Curtis "50 Cent" Jackson. There's another story where Alphabet City invested nearly their entire marketing budget on an exclusive pair of New York Yankees on-the-field seats. This opportunity brought about a chance meeting with our boy Jay-Z, and then splitting those tickets with him for the next decade. It was all just business, man. Pretty valuable friendships to make, but it underscores the lesson in life that you make your own luck by taking risks and being in the right place at the right time. It's the story of Jesse's success and life.

MARQUIS JET

Jesse and his partner then sell off Alphabet City for $5 million and got a taste of the high life shortly thereafter—riding in a NetJets private jet. Seeing that this is an experience out of reach for most, he thinks about how to make private jet travel more "available" for the mass affluent and celebrities. Fast-forward to a meeting with the NetJets president, who flatly turns down their idea of lowering his leasing increments from five years to as low as 25 hours with a card, like Starbucks.

He gets another meeting a week later, but this time shows up with some of his personal connections just waiting to rent jet hours. Among them: a Giant's NFL player, members of a rap group, a well-known NBA agent, and a successful Wall Street guy. SOLD.

Take notes on this and below: that's a masterclass on how to pitch a product. Create a problem and solve it: Entrepreneurship 101. Successful businesses go beyond the pitch though. They have to get real results; here's how Jesse got them. They needed deep-pocketed clientele for Marquis Jet, so he looked to the ultra-wealthy in Silicon Valley and double-downed on the celebrity market.

GOT MUFFINS?

How do you get access to pitch your product to the Silicon Valley elite? Jesse discovered TED talks (Technology, Entertainment, and Design). They were just starting up in San Francisco then, and not as commonplace as they are today. The problem for him was that you needed a lanyard to get in, and he didn't have one. What was his angle to get in?

Jesse's answer was a stake out, as in across the street. He noticed the local coffee place was packed with people wearing those same TED lanyards every morning. Guess what they ordered? A coffee and a muffin to go. You can't stop the coffee from flowing, but you could corner the muffin market.

So, the next morning, Jesse was first in line for the coffee shop, bought every last muffin, and sat in the corner. When a lanyard would walk in and ask for a coffee and muffin, the barista would say,

"Coffee here, free muffins over there." The first gentleman to walk over was a newly minted billionaire, and asked Jesse,

"What do you do?" Jesse responded:

"I own my own private jet company." The other gentleman replied,

"What are the chances? I'm in the market for one of those."

What are the chances? You have to hustle and make your own luck in life.

IT'S WHO YOU KNOW, NOT WHAT YOU KNOW

Every morning, Jesse and his team got an emailed flight itinerary for those who were flying that day on NetJets private jets. He was in New York City when he noticed Matt Damon and Ben Affleck's names on the list flying from LAX. Their destination was the Sundance Film Festival, flying in an upgraded business class jet outfitted with a bedroom and conference room- more than enough room for the six people booked. He immediately booked a one-way ticket to LAX, with only 45 minutes to spare to meet Matt and Ben at the hanger. He then asked if he could ride on the jump seat and would return the favor. They said "OK", and using this opportunity, signed them both up for Marquis Jet Cards. How'd he get home? Doesn't matter—new connections were made, and new friendships were born.

Guess what other celebrity contacts eventually became Marquis Jet card carriers? If you guessed Jay-Z and 50 Cent you'd be correct. They remembered Jesse from their experiences with him at Alphabet City and signed up because of their friendships. Are you getting the point here? It's who you know, not what you know.

Enter the best connection of his life: a Marquis Jet invite-only client appreciation poker event, where Sara Blakely of Spanx was attending. Being both successful entrepreneurs in their thirties and single, the two hit it off. Months later they began dating, eventually married, and created a beautiful family of six in no time. Always remember, the personal connections you make can pay dividends in more ways than one down the road- especially love, the biggest prize in life. Protect and foster relationships with the right people.

ATHLETE, INVESTOR, AUTHOR, AND OWNER

After an extremely profitable 10-year run, Jesse and his partners sell Marquis Jet to Warren Buffet's Berkshire Hathaway. The selling price isn't disclosed, but Jesse becomes a rich entrepreneur with a lot of energy and means. He ventures into ultramarathons, discovering that coconut water is the best electrolyte beverage he could consume during his 100-mile endurance run. What do you think he does next? That's right, he partners with a small coconut water company, called Zico, and then a clever stunt with Matt Damon (you can look it up), it gets sold to Coca-Cola within three years for a hefty premium. Again, it's who you know, not what you know.

He then went on to become a New York Times Best-selling author twice over for Living with a Seal, where he lived and trained with "The World's Toughest Man", David Goggins; and then the follow-up book Living with the Monks.

For the encore? In 2015, he and his billionaire wife were part of a group that purchased the Atlanta Hawks for $850 million. Winning in business and life is where anything is possible if you just ask (his mantra).

He has accomplished so much, but his social feed is filled with his and Sara's family they created, and celebrating the moments they soak in together. I respect the hell out of that more than any of either's business accomplishments. I have to believe that even a celebrity's family comes first, but Jesse and Sara seem to live it. I'd assume the same for Jay-Z and Beyonce's family of five, but being kept private, no one knows for sure. Money can always be earned, but the time you have here is limited. Once you find success, don't forget how you got there. Get your priorities right and enjoy your time with your loved ones.

Hustle, talent, vision, and wisdom only get you so far as a successful entrepreneur. If you want this for yourself, then strap in for the ride and be willing to pivot, be creative, and be open to new ideas and connections as life unfolds.

Let's sum this chapter up with an entrepreneur's business plan.

– THE "JUST GET STARTED " BUSINESS PLAN –

Think you have what it takes to be an entrepreneur? My journey to entrepreneurship started with the question, "How?"

During my college internship at Merril Lynch, I got to work under a very successful, female financial advisor. She anchored a thriving corner office in an industry dominated by pale, stale, and male types. She taught me how to stand out, communicate, and be in control of my client's best interests. Do a professional job and you'll be respected. Don't be caught playing golf five days a week. I wanted her corner office job, the power, the money, the influence, and even the stress she endured during the dot-com bubble burst. No matter what, she was always calm and in control.

I got a taste, and I wanted to be "that advisor" someday.

If you're asking yourself how someone has something in life you want, ask questions. Fuel your passion with a way to escape your current situation like Eminem did. Stay curious and get an internship like 50 Cent. Be willing to work and hustle like Jay-Z did selling CDs out of the back of the car. Create your own luck like Jesse Itzler has his entire life.

I didn't have to start my own record label, but I had to build a book of business (clients who paid me a fee) from zero. This is a Catch 22- you need clients, but you don't have what they require: experience. No one is giving their life savings to a 23-year-old who hasn't lived through any ups and downs of the stock market. Just like how Jay-Z didn't start one of his first successful business ventures, Rocawear, without any hits first, or Jesse Itzler building Marquis Jet without the connections he made and developed.

The hustle of "making it" can be seen in the eyes of those who've done it prior. You will fail a lot, but every time you do, you're not starting over—you're starting from experience.
Walking through those coals makes every obstacle easier in life.

This can be hastened by internships, where you can gain experience from a pro as I had at Merrill Lynch in college, or like Jay-Z being Big Daddy Kane's hype man. It can be improved through collaborations, like when I did marketing with other advisors to spread costs and opportunities evenly. Just like Roc-a-fella's three founding members collaborated in the beginning. Throw in some hustle, like Jay-Z selling CDs out of the back of his car, then it's only a matter of time before you make your own luck.

What's your niche? Have you discovered a problem and learned how to solve it? If not, there's no business there. That's why experience under another pro is always the best move when you're younger—learn what they've learned about that particular industry. Sometimes the problem lies in scarcity—not enough people providing a service or good. Other times it's quality—too many people doing a subpar job. No need to reinvent the circle, just make it your circle. You don't need any special qualifications to put on a smile, network, be punctual, or be respectful. If you don't have these desires or a niche, it's best to work for someone who does.

Once you've learned, now you can earn. Starting your entrepreneurial business from nothing is a thankless process, costing hours of your life by convincing yourself and your business into existence.

"Started From The Bottom" by Drake is your soundtrack.

> **❝** *Boys tell stories 'bout the man*
> *Say I never struggled, wasn't hungry, yeah, I doubt it, n****a*
> *I could turn your boy into the man*
> *There ain't really much I hear that's poppin' off without us, n****a*
> *We just want the credit where it's due*
> *I'ma worry 'bout me, give a f*ck about you*
> *N****a, just as a reminder to myself*
> *I wear every single chain, even when I'm in the house.* **❞**

I worked hard and made great money at my college lawn irrigation job. But, the glass ceiling at a small company isn't very high. Knowing job opportunities were slim after college and having dreams of getting back into financial services from my internship days, I made a decision to just get started.

There's never a good time to do anything, so I naively saved up what I thought I'd need to get by for a few months—a laughable $2,000. After I passed my securities exams, I had a few sit-down meetings with former lawn irrigation clients. From making sure their lawns were green to managing their green? Outcome: "thank you for your time young man and best of luck."

I'm sure Jesse could have figured that pivot out better than me, and Em or Jay could make it flow, but I couldn't find any work or clients. I had no family help either, and the debt started piling up. Only a misunderstood email reply got my foot in the door, with a local fire department from the offer of "free pizzas for all—no strings attached." It took three years of toiling away to find my niche and make it into the financial advisor business.

The Struggle Gives You Purpose™. What doesn't kill you makes you stronger. 50 Cent got shot nine times and got back up, but no one's asking you to do the same. The mistakes you make along the way are the best teacher—even better than an actual mentor showing you the ropes. You have to learn how to fly and fall on your face a few times. If you can get back up and try again, then you have what it takes to be an entrepreneur. If not, go get that steady paycheck, time off, and health insurance. The first time you screw up and can't provide for yourself or your family, will show you meddle. If you can just keep going, you'll make sure those mistakes don't happen again and get back to "tryin to make $1 outta 15 cents".

THEN

Repeat. The easiest part of business: just repeat what you've discovered to fill your niche a thousand more times. If you love it, you won't get bored. If you've had to earn it, the steak will taste better. If you have to provide for others, you will feel a responsibility of giving back. You can always re-tool the process to be faster, more efficient, cost you less; but don't sacrifice your quality. As an entrepreneur, you're in the quality business (Corporations are in the quantity business), but you can make a lot of money doing what you love through repetition.

Here's simple math on how to make a million dollars:
Whatever business you're in dictates the formula you should use.
Selling records? Need 1,000,000 people. Selling financial advice? Then
you only need 1,000 people. Different scales for different sales. Know
your niche and provide the quality someone else doesn't.

– HOW to MAKE $1 Milli! –

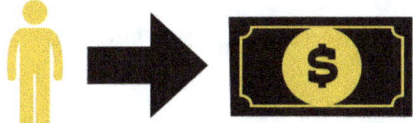

FIND **1,000** PEOPLE TO PAY YOU **$1,000**

=**1000**
PEOPLE

=**$1000**

FIND **10,000** PEOPLE TO PAY YOU **$100**

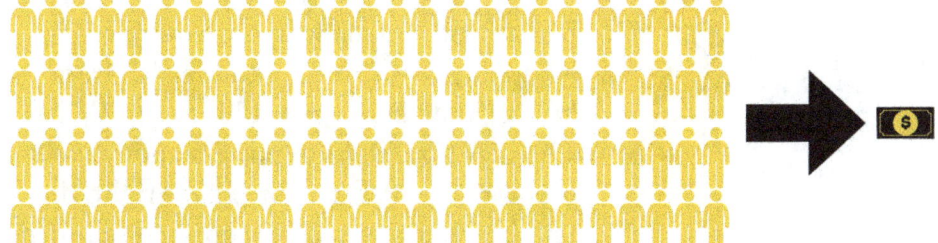

FIND **100,000** TO PAY YOU **$10**

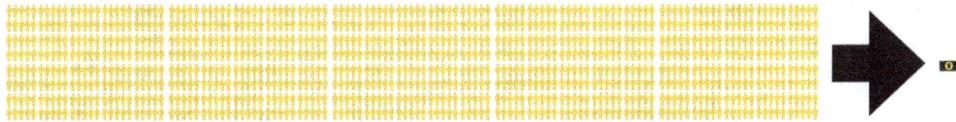

FIND **1,000,000** PEOPLE TO PAY YOU **$1**

DON'T FORGET

The worst part of being an entrepreneur is running the actual business.
You found a niche business for your passion? Check.
You set up your website, social channels, and people are noticing you.
Check-check.

You found out you're really good at said business and making some
money. Check-chiggity-check.

Great for you! You took that leap into entrepreneurship and showed
the world what you can do.

While your personal bank account is getting fatter, one day you get a
notice about this thing called "taxes". Wait, what? This is my money I
earned legally all by myself. Why do I have to pay taxes to the Feds,
State-ys, and local yocals? Because you do.

Al Capone famously said after being convicted of tax evasion: "They
can't collect legal taxes from illegal money!" Oh yes, the Internal
Revenue Service (IRS) can and will- legal and illegal monies. It doesn't
matter what kind of business you're running, slinging crack rock or a
wicked jump shot, not turning in a tax
return will cost you dearly.

> "They can't collect
> legal taxes from
> illegal money!"
> -Al Capone

Just ask Lil' Wayne who once owed a
whopping $14.2 million to the IRS from
two separate liens against his assets. What's
a lien? A legal right to possess another's
property to satisfy a debt. That's right, the
IRS can take your possessions and sell them
to make them whole.

How'd it happen?

My guess is poor business management of earned income while he was
busy being a performer, sipping on champagne, and throwing up bills
at the club. Some artists get ripped off by their management and others

get ripped off by their management not doing their jobs correctly.

One more time for the people in the back- invest in the right people.

Fortunately for Lil' Wayne, he had the right friend with deep pockets; a Mr. Shawn "Jay-Z" Carter who came in and reportedly "helped him out" (sorry, no details to disclose). Lil' Wayne got in trouble with the IRS because he was busy doing what he loved and raking in millions. How can that be a crime? Because he didn't stay up on his taxes.

The worst part of being an entrepreneur is running the actual business.

Just like all entrepreneurs getting started and trying to make a business out of what they love to do, I've made these similar missteps but can share with you now my golden rules.

– FOUR ENTREPRENEUR GOLDEN RULES –

1. SET UP AN LLC

It stands for Limited Liability Company. As it sounds, this is to legally limit and protect your personal stuff (assets) from any business problems (losses). Guess what happens if you don't? You'll have "99 problems and a b*tch ain't one."

Let's say you've got an ice cream business and forgot to separate out your personal and business assets. Life is sweet until a kid gets sick, then a parent, then another—turns out you were selling listeria-tainted ice cream. Your business gets shut down by health officials and you're being sued. Game over rover, you'll lose all your assets and your dreams. Moral of the story, get an LLC and proper business insurance.
How do you set an LLC up? Easy as A-B-C.

A. You'll need a unique name,
B. Pay a state filing fee, and then
C. Create a TIN (Tax Identification Number) with the IRS (free).

Once you have all three, head to your bank and open up a business bank account with your info. Consider opening up a business credit card too and separate all your income and expenses.

2. BOOKKEEPING SOFTWARE

The single worst part of a business is accounting. Accounts receivable, debits and credits, inventory, cost of goods sold, keeping track of your mileage, etc., etc. There's a reason why rappers like accountants to count their stacks.

From "Juicy" by Notorious B.I.G.:

> **"**Got two rides, a limousine with a chauffeur. Phone bill about two G's flat. No need to worry, my accountant handles that.**"**

From "R.I.C.O" by Meek Mill ft. Drake:

> **"**I've been counted out so many times, I couldn't count it. Funny how now my accountant is havin' trouble tryna count it**"**

From "All I Do Is Win" by DJ Khaled ft. Ludacris, Rick Ross, T-Pain & Snoop Dogg:

> **"**Got twenty bank accounts, accountants count me in. Make millions every year, the south's champion**"**

You definitely should invest in a good accountant like B.I.G. did or Drake does, but when you're just starting out, use a great accounting app on your phone.

My go-to is the QuickBooks Self-employed app. It's a monthly subscription, but pound for pound, does a great job for the price. It automatically tracks the mileage you drive, as well as keeps track of all your income and expenses coming in through your business. All you need to do is go through and tap your business miles vs. personal (not deductible) and categorize your bank transactions into meals, office expenses, travel, utilities, etc. The trick is to do this weekly, or you'll get behind.

Guess what? When it's tax time, you can either share your data with a real accountant or buy QuickBooks tax software. Done.

3. THE 30% RULE
Let's say you do numbers one and two and don't pull a Capone or Lil' Wayne. Your tax software says you owe the IRS money because you didn't pay these things called "quarterly taxes" on your "1099 income". For you beginners out there, 1099 income is paid directly to you, with no taxes held back. Now, it sounds great making 100%, but that's not all yours because of… that's right, taxes.

Always save back 30% of what you make because you'll owe federal, state, local, and the biggest surprise for most: self-employment (SE) taxes. What's SE taxes? This is key: you're the employer and employee, so you have to pay twice. Read it and weep, or just save back 30%.

4. MENTORS / PARTNERS / FRIENDS
You may think being an entrepreneur is going it alone, but you'll have partners along the way who can teach you the game, share ideas, and spread out the risk.

Jay-Z had two other partners starting Roc-a-fella Records, Jesse Itzler had one other at Alphabet City and Marquis Jet, and I'd bet both had mentors to learn from as well.

When I started out smiling-and-dialing in the bullpen at the first firm I worked at, I met one of my best friends. We've shared so many business ideas, dreams, and off-work fun over the past 20 years. It's essential. He's better at the things I'm not and vice versa. He loves golf and I'd rather be skiing. But we both love our careers, watching sports, and hip-hop. Have someone in your business life that pushes you and shares their successes. It's the abundance mindset: there's plenty to go around, so share what's working. When we all win, we all win together.

HELP!

Speaking of winning together, at some point you're going to need more help than meeting a buddy for a beer after work. Especially if you're a solo entrepreneur with no partners. You're going to need help in your business to make it what it can be; so, hire help. No different than when Snoop Dogg, Eminem, and 50 Cent got signed and hired Dr. Dre as their producer; you need to build a team that's the right fit for you.

ADDING EMPLOYEES

Human capital will cost you a lot of money, but at this point in the game, you'll understand what your time is worth. This is when you'll decide to focus on what you do best, rather than all the chores that come with being a successful entrepreneur.

I've offered internships before, but making the decision to add an assistant was a game changer: no more paperwork or scheduling meetings. Adding my second assistant changed my life: allowing me to truly be flexible in my personal and business life.

The biggest lesson I had to learn was no one is great at everything, even a solo- entrepreneur. Rolling solo, you have to wear all the hats. Deciding to take off a few hats is exactly that—you're allowing another person to do that work for you. It's easy to get frustrated that this person can't be as motivated as you, or as good at multitasking as you, or as [fill in the blank], but I guarantee they're great at a few things you can leverage in your business, so look past any flaws.

Pay people what they're worth and treat them with respect. If you happen to find just the right person for just the right fit, you had better prioritize keeping them happy and paid. An upset or let down employee will make your business suffer and multiply problems. If you can't offer a generous salary, make it up with bonuses as you hit goals, vacation time, and other perks common now, like remote work. Money is only a tool—true employer-employee happiness comes from being an understanding boss; flexible, caring, and then generous with time and cash. That's what makes the business run and churn out hits!

CONSIDERING A PARTNER?

Finding the right people (again!) to surround you and your business with is almost as important as picking the right spouse. My dad always told me that a partnership is a marriage with no love. Truer words were never spoken. Try being cordial with a business partner when both of you are stressed out, frustrated, trying to pay bills on time, and trying to keep your customers happy. You need a fellow business professional that you trust and are completely in alignment with.

You two should also be complementary- meaning you both have different skill sets that play off each other. It's that same exact rule with a rapper (Snoop, Em, and 50) and a producer (Dre). When it works, magic can happen. When it doesn't, it's a flop. It's a huge shift; going from being solo to a team workplace, so check your ego, be open to new ideas, and focus on your tasks within the partnership. Remember to have fun.

That's the reason you went on this journey, so make sure to share it with your team. Celebrate the wins you all worked hard for. Use every win as an opportunity to reward and then reset your team goals.

What do you do when things don't go right? It's even more important to take a moment and blow off steam. You have to get offsite to do something non-work related that's fun and at the least, relaxing. It's important to blow off steam and take a break. Create an opportunity to show your team you care for them, regardless of what didn't go right with your business that day or week.

Hip-hop's most recognized top old-school producer and founder of Def Jam, Rick Rubin, had to find a way to extract such hits from talents such as "No Sleep Till Brooklyn" (Beastie Boys), "Walk this Way" (Run D.M.C/Aerosmith), and "99 Problems" (Jay-Z). He started off producing artists like LL Cool J, turning his dorm room at NYU into Def Jam's first studio and office (in true entrepreneurship style).

In his now-famous 60 Minutes interview, he was asked if he played any instruments.

"Barely". Anderson Cooper then asks, "You must know something," to which he responds,

"Well, I know what I like and what I don't like. And I'm decisive about what I like and what I don't like."

Huh?

After being pressed about how exactly he's been able to produce and extract so many legendary hits for so many different artists, at unique times in their lives, he replied that his sole talent is,

"The confidence that I have in my taste and my ability to express what I feel has proven helpful for artists."

Hey, whatever works for you and your team, but you need someone to sense when there's a problem or when something goes right. I'm betting a huge part of Rick's producer success is keeping his artists happy and honest. That's real talent.

STAY ABOARD OR JUMP-OFF?

Every beginning has an end, but in business, you're either growing or you're dying. The adventure of starting your own business is a financial and emotional roller coaster ride of wild twists and turns. The process of learning, earning, and then growing your team to hundreds, or keeping it a small boutique, is one completely unique to you. You may decide you like the challenge of going for an IPO, or the fun and looseness of a small team.

At some point though, after you've survived the first five years, the most crucial thing in any business: you have to think about a long-term plan, because your people—your family, your partners, your employees, and your clients all depend on you. Data from the Bureau of Labor Statistics (BLS) shows that approximately 20% of new businesses fail during the first two years of being open, 45% during the first five years, and 65% during the first 10 years. Only 25% of new businesses make it to 15 years or more. If you survive those stats, or simply your life and interests change, you need a plan. As said in the financial planning business: failure to have a plan is planning to fail.

1. You can always stay small and have fun. Money isn't everything, right? This is your true independent entrepreneur. How I started my business from nothing to something.

For hip-hop, think: Macklemore, Mac Miller (deceased), Chance the Rapper, Too-Short, and E-40. They do it for the love of the game and make some bank along the way. A win-win for both your passion and business.

2. You can scale up and grow, but do you really want to lose your small company vibes for a large company bureaucracy? For me, I'm an independent financial advisor, but as my business grew, I moved up the food chain into larger broker-dealers (that's finance talk for regulatory compliance) who allowed for both independence (I'm not told what to sell; I choose what's best for my clients), and they let me be me, plus the pay-outs are much better. I've added to my team, but still remain a small, boutique firm. Just the way I like it.

For Dre, Snoop, and 2pac, it was Death Row Records. For Biggie, it was Bad Boy Records. For Drake, it was Cash Money Records. Every other successful rapper they scale up by getting dined, signed, and then grind for larger organizations that have a national and international reach to promote and then sell their art.

3. You can bring on a strategic partner to share in the wins and losses. Cases in point: Kanye partnered his Yeezy Brand with Adidas and got paid 15% royalty on all sales. It was his vision and sales techniques, but strategically Adidas's expertise that was used in making and distributing his shoes.

Jesse Itzler partnered his Marquis Jet with NetJets, using their jets to lease out in smaller, more lucrative increments. He then proceeded to #4 for an undisclosed sum, but probably eight zeros and two commas.

4. You can sell out and get paid. Every entrepreneur has the same independent interest, but some enjoy starting businesses or buying existing ones to scale them up and then sell them off. It's "All About the Benjamins" and I won't hate these generational wealth sums that were created.

Dr. Dre and Jimmy Iovine started Beats Headphones. They sold it to Apple in 2014 for a reported $3 billion with his after-tax cash-out check at around $500 million. Good thing they went into speakers instead of sneakers.

Jay-Z acquired the Armand de Brignac "Ace of Spades" ultra-premium champagne (save that gold bottle for personal recycling!) in 2014. In 2021, he reportedly sold 50% of the champagne business to LVMH's Moët Hennessy for an estimated $315 million. I'm sure he celebrated with a magnum bottle of their finest. Honorable mention: he also bought Tidal, a music streaming service, for $56 million in 2015 and then sold it for $297 million in 2021 as well.

Whatever journey you go on as an entrepreneur, you get to decide the outcome. That's the point and the best part. Do what's best for you, your family, your partners, and your employees; but never forget about the clients that believe in you.

TAKE ACTION!

THREE-FOURS!

FOUR WAYS TO MAKE MONEY:

1. EMPLOYED
2. SELF-EMPLOYED,
3. REAL ESTATE
4. INVESTOR

FOUR ENTREPRENEUR GOLDEN RULES

1. SET-UP AN LLC
2. BOOK-KEEPING SOFTWARE
3. THE 30% RULE
4. MENTORS, PARTNERS, & FRIENDS

FOUR LONG-TERM PLANS

1. STAY SMALL AND HAVE FUN.
2. SCALE UP AND GROW.
3. BRING ON A STRATEGIC PARTNER TO SHARE THE WINS AND LOSSES.
4. SELL OUT AND GET PAID.

- END OF TRACK 3 -

track 4.

MO' MONEY, MO' PROBLEMS

TRACK 4: MO' MONEY, MO' PROBLEMS

> *"I don't know what they want from me,*
> *It's like the mo' money we come across,*
> *The mo' problems we see."*

-Notorious B.I.G. "Mo' Money, Mo' Problems"

You struggle. You hustle. You learn. You earn. You deserve to treat yourself to everything you can afford, right?

Wrong.

There's a reason we started out this book with the dramatic rise and fall of MC Hammer. As any rapper coming from nothing would stereotypically do; get a million-dollar advance, spend the million-dollar advance. If it comes quick, it leaves quick; just like every lottery winner or most people who inherit money.

Here are a couple of real-life tracks from the double album of life. When I hired my assistant straight out of college, she saw her first-ever annual salary and wanted to, nobly, do her part to save the environment.

How? She wanted to buy a Tesla. She forgot to deduct taxes from her bi-monthly check and discovered she was coming up way too short every month to pay her rent, utilities, and food. Wine taste, beer money? She opted for an eco-friendly Compact Jeep. She has an emergency savings account and is maxing out her tax-free ROTH IRA investment account every month. I am very proud of her and know she's got a great future ahead.

On the flip side, I've helped hundreds of clients retire. What do you think the most common request is? After working [blank] years, I want to [fill in the blank] for me and [fill in the blank]. Every retiree wants to treat themselves, and those they love around them, to something really nice when they hang up their cleats. Be it a new vacation home they want to split half their time at, a collector's car that takes them back to their childhood years, an entire extended family Disney trip, or that bucket list trip they've been dreaming of for years, there's always a big purchase. Usually, it's all good as long as we plan it out. Sometimes it's a bit more than someone can bite off and we re-evaluate, or they disagree, do it anyways, and are impacted for the rest of their life.

We're going to drill down on everyone's worst nightmare when they walk into my office: the dreaded budget conversation. It doesn't matter if you're just starting out or end-of-career, you need one to get ahead. So many people float through for decades and then struggle when they don't want to work anymore. Knowing what one spends every month on essentials and non-essentials determines what you can save—really easy math. Does a financial planner care what you spend money on? Absolutely not! We all have our own preferences, goals, and dreams. So, who am I, or another financial planner, to tell you "No." Unless you're spending too much on non-essentials and not enough on your goals. Then we have a talk about what's the most important and cut back from the bottom of your list. Period. End-of-story.

I could end the chapter now, but here's Ice Cube's advice: "Stop buying things you don't need, to impress people you don't like with money you don't have." We can throw on our marketing hats and call it "inflows" and "outflows" if it makes you feel better, but it's still a budget and it's all about your cash—as in cash flow. If you can master your cash flow, you will fly high and far.

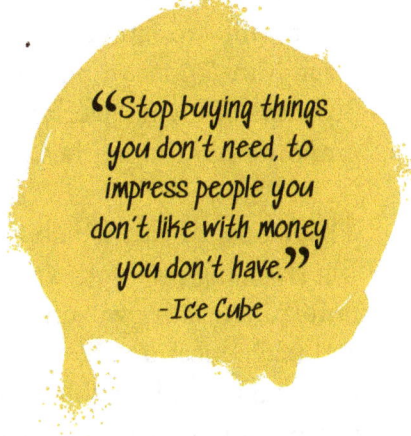

> "Stop buying things you don't need, to impress people you don't like with money you don't have."
> -Ice Cube

If you don't, then you just may end up

filing for Chapter 11 personal bankruptcy like MC Hammer or Donald Trump, or our next real-life example: 50 Cent.

As a former intern for Jesse Itzler at Alphabet Records learning the art of the hustle, how exactly does the student surpass the teacher by more than double his net worth, only to nearly lose it all? By 2007, 50 Cent had gotten all the way to the number two spot on Forbes wealthiest rapper list, with a nearly $500 million net worth—only behind to, now-billionaire, Jay-Z. You can blame circumstances, bad business decisions, legal quandaries, and excessive risk-taking; but he didn't have control over his monthly cash flow. Ultimately, the same two words that brought down the Hammer landed 50 in personal bankruptcy: House-poor. Where the things you own, own you.

Here's a brief story you probably don't know of the struggle, hustle, learning, and earning Curtis Jackson III went through to become the 50 Cent you know.

– 50'S COME UP –

Curtis Jackson III grew up in the New York City borough of Queens, in the neighborhood of Little Jamaica. His mother was a drug dealer and passed away when he was only eight years old. His grandparents had to step up and raise him. It's an unfortunate circumstance for any child to be in, but he had learned adversity at a young age. It's a terrible story to write, let alone live, and I can't imagine the hole left in him to try and fill. No father, and then no mother, to be a parent for him, to teach him- and love him. As a father and knowing the absolute 24/7, 365 days of loving-work that goes into a child, I'd like to think his grandmother did her best, but the streets became his teacher.

That's how he learned about life, finance, and the hustling business. Big risks, big pay-outs, and then big spending. It's the same unfortunate story woven through the fabric of hip-hop: home-stability and real education are absent and nature's rules- survival of the fittest- reign supreme. I feel blessed that I was afforded the basics by my parents, and that I wasn't left to fend for myself.

When Curtis was 11, he found a place to take out his aggression and fill that void: the boxing ring. However, within a year, young Curtis was out on the street hustling and selling drugs. Fast forward to 18, he lands an internship with Jesse Itzler, trying to break into the music biz, and meets Jam Master J of Run DMC. Within a year, his street hustle catches up to him, resulting in him getting arrested twice in three weeks for drugs and guns.

Convicted for three-to-six years, he entered a prison boot camp over a six-month period and earned his GED. Serving as a wake-up call, when he was released, he adopted the moniker of "50 Cent" to symbolize literal change- as well as pay homage to the 1980s Brooklyn robber with the same name.

Now focused, he honed his lyrical skills in a friend's basement. Within two years he gets his introduction to Jam Master Jay; presumably through his prior relationship with Jesse. He gets signed to Jam Master Jay's label, learns the ways of rap, and leaves for Columbia Records to work on his debut record.

He then released his first successful, intentionally controversial, underground single, "How to Rob". On it, he comically describes how he would rob famous rappers like Jay-Z, Big Pun, DMX, and the Wu-Tang Clan, amongst others. All clap back at the up-and-comer, gaining him attention and landing him a spot-on Nas's Nastradamus tour.

Soon after he gets dropped from Columbia and blacklisted by the recording industry because of another controversial song, "Ghetto Qu'ran". This time it went too far into calling out his past gang relations; presumably the ones that got him infamously shot nine times in front of his poor grandmother, with his young son in the house. Any dreams for fame and breaking out of the ghetto are almost erased. Against all odds, he survives, and heads north to Canada for a couple of years, releasing mixtape after mixtape.

You should know the rest of the story from here: Eminem takes him to

LA to meet Dre, they sign him for a cool $1 million, released "In Da Club" off his major label debut Get Rich or Die Tryin, and 50 Cent becomes a household name.

– MO' MONEY, MO' SPENDING –

Earning a lot of money gives some people the license to spend a lot of money. After all, coming from absolutely nothing to hundreds of millions in the bank is the same rags-to-riches story of Brooklyn boxing prodigy "Iron Mike" Tyson. He also had no control over his monthly cash flow and his over-the-top lifestyle saw him piss-away lifetime earnings of over $400 million!

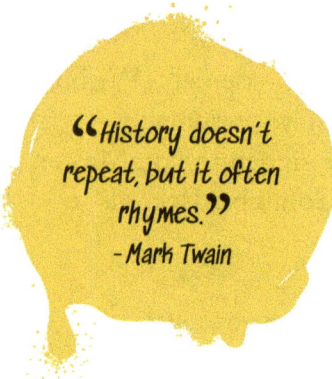

"History doesn't repeat, but it often rhymes."
- Mark Twain

Just like Mark Twain's famous line, "History doesn't repeat, but it often rhymes", 50 fell into the same trap "Iron Mike" did. Using some of the $38 million in profits from his breakout album and subsequent tour, he moved out of the ghetto and bought "Iron Mike's" former 55,000-square-foot mansion in Farmington, Connecticut for $4.1 million. Where had he been prior? Struggling to pay his $800-a-month rent bill for the apartment he shared with his then-partner and his first son, Marquise.

Quick math lesson: 50 is on the record saying that the annual upkeep bill was a cool $700,000 or $67,000. Per. Month. Now times that by the length of time he owned it for, 14 years, and that's a staggering $9.8 million just to maintain it. That's well over twice what he paid for it.

Enter Jay-Z quote: "If you can't buy it twice, you can't afford it". The things you own can own you if you don't keep your mind on your money.

"If you can't buy it twice, you can't afford it."
- Jay-Z

His money is cash-flowing out of his palace while he's on tour. Fortunately, in this period of superstardom, 50 is bringing in way mo' money than his lavish spending.

His business acumen shines when he nets an $80 million, five-year deal with Reebok. His follow-up act is striking lightning in a bottle of Vitamin Water. Taking no pay and opting instead for shares in the company to promote the brand, he rides Formula 50 to the bank for over a $100-million-dollar payday (after-taxes!) when Coca-Cola buys Vitamin Water for $4.1 billion in 2007.

Life works out until it doesn't.

- BAD DECISIONS -

We all got hit by the Great Financial Crisis in 2008-2009. Successful or not, you're always one bad recession and downturn away from bad money mistakes catching up to you. That's why the first rule in budgeting is minding your cash flow and keeping an adequate cash account before investing.

The hits dried up as fame always does, but 50's spending remained the same. A great rule in life: never spend money to keep up appearances.

Wealth is quiet. Rich is loud. Poor is flashy.

In 2011, he tried to cash in like Dr. Dre by releasing his own headphones. Ultimately this proves to be a failed business attempt and loses him a big $18 million. Ouch. The life of an entrepreneur is taking risks. Sometimes they work out and other times you lose, but you should always be learning. Just as the streets taught him in his childhood: take big risks, if you want big pay-outs, and then you can have big spending. All true until it isn't. He takes the "L" on the risk and payout, but his spending remains the same.

A year later, 50 becomes a dad again with girlfriend, and model, Daphne Narvaez to a son, Sire. The relationship doesn't last and then child support payments commence to a tune of $12,100 per month. Queue Kanye from "Gold Digger":

> *"Eighteen years, eighteen years*
> *She got one of your kids, got you for eighteen years*
> *I know somebody payin' child support for one of his kids*
> *His baby mama car and crib is bigger than his..."*

Fun fact: This type of debt doesn't go away even when you file for personal bankruptcy protection.

Kids: invest in the right person you want to become a potential parent with.

To top off the bad decision hit list, we get to 50's feuds and legal troubles. It's one thing to have a disagreement, it's a whole other thing to have manufactured a feud to sell more records (2pac v. Biggie or 50 v. Kanye), but it's entirely a bad decision to post someone's personal life on the internet without their consent. You're going to get sued and if you're a person of means, you're already a target, so you're going to get sued for millions. You have to use that brain God gave you and not allow yourself to make stupid decisions.

It's no secret he and rap nemesis Rick Ross have had a long feud dating back to the mid-2000s and is still going strong to this day. Sinking to a new low, 50 gets his hands on a personal sex tape of Rick Ross's ex-girlfriend and posts it on the internet. She sues him and wins a $7 million legal judgement. That's a slam dunk victory and what proved to be the nail in the coffin for 50 to pursue Chapter 11 personal bankruptcy protection.

Total cumulative legal fees for 50: at least $23 million. Bad decisions will always catch up to you. Especially on top of not minding your mouth, money, and cash flow.

THE THINGS YOU OWN, CAN OWN YOU.

One of the biggest misconceptions in investing is thinking a house is an appreciating asset only— an asset whose value can go up over time. You definitely want to invest in appreciating assets, but it can also be one of your biggest liabilities by sucking your cash flow dry every month. Especially if it's 55,000 square feet, 21 bedrooms, 24 bathrooms, and a nightclub requiring massive upkeep costs. That's not a home, that's opulence that drove not one, but two superstars to bankruptcy.

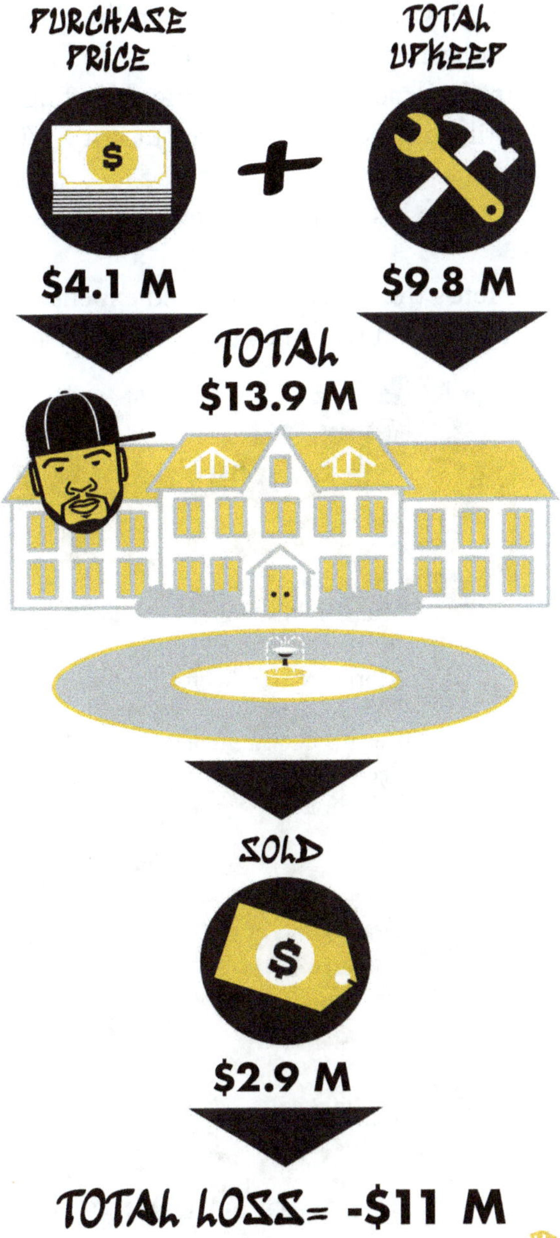

When buying a house, you have to consider not only the mortgage, but also the upkeep (utilities), planned costs (remodeling), and the surprise costs (AC unit, hot water heater, etc.) that will happen over a long period of time. Mortgages usually start at a 30-year term, so you have to plan ahead for the long term, even if you don't stay in that home for that length of time.

For 50, he could easily afford his mansion when the times were fat, but after 14 years of the $700,000 annual upkeep bill ($9.8 million), he had to sell at a steep loss, only $2.9 million. A far cry from when he first listed the property for sale in 2007 at $18.5 million.

Ouch.

PURCHASE PRICE

TOTAL UPKEEP

$4.1 M   +   **$9.8 M**

TOTAL $13.9 M

SOLD

$2.9 M

TOTAL LOSS= -$11 M

Not all homes are investments. Hopefully the new owners aren't the superstar of the moment and keeping their mind on their money.

CHAPTER 11 PERSONAL BANKRUPTCY

Just like Hammer and "Iron Mike" before him, Curtis "50 Cent" Jackson III filed for Chapter 11 personal bankruptcy protection in 2015 with a debt of -$32.5 million to resolve. In his case, he didn't go broke, but he had lost a substantial amount of his net worth (- $440M) in the process of getting there, leaving him with around $30 million. Still considered very rich, but not $470 million rich.

Besides his property upkeep, what else made up his lavish lifestyle?

Here's the actual "household expenses" from his bankruptcy record, and a lesson on what not to spend every month.

HOUSEHOLD EXPENSES

		MONTHLY
CT	Gardening	5,000
	Household supplies	1,500
	Insurance-Homeowners	13,300
	Mortgage (P,I & Property tax	17,400
	Pool Maintenance	1,500
	Repairs & Maintenance	4,500
	Security & Protection	9,000
	Telephone	600
	Utilities	14,200
		67,000
GA	HOA Dues (3286 Northside Pkwy)	1,100
	Property Taxes	400
	Utilities	200
		1,700
NJ	Rent	3,000
	Utilities	300
		3,300
	TOTAL HOUSEHOLD EXPENSES	**$72,000**

In order, from high to low, just like any good financial planner would create; a budget:

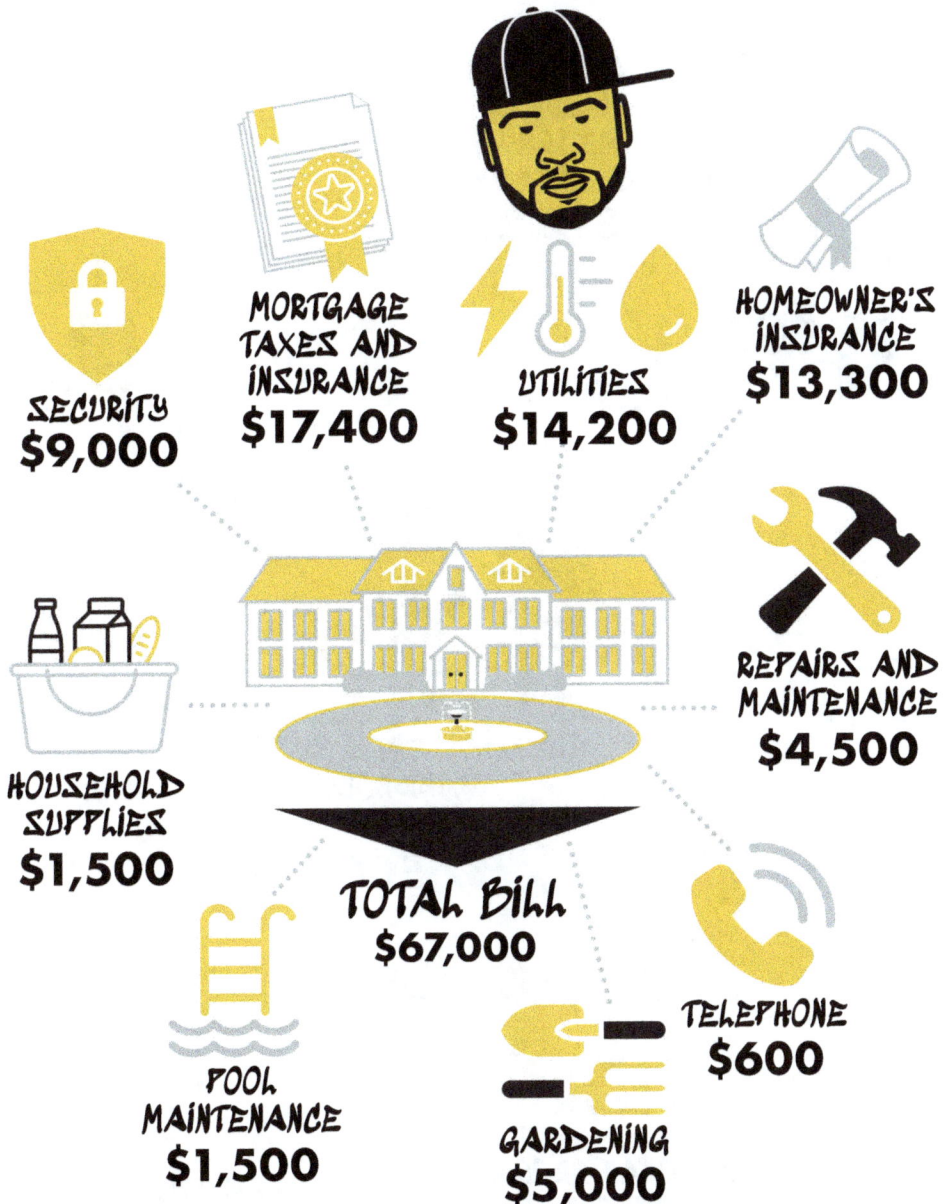

SECURITY $9,000

MORTGAGE TAXES AND INSURANCE $17,400

UTILITIES $14,200

HOMEOWNER'S INSURANCE $13,300

HOUSEHOLD SUPPLIES $1,500

REPAIRS AND MAINTENANCE $4,500

TOTAL BILL $67,000

POOL MAINTENANCE $1,500

GARDENING $5,000

TELEPHONE $600

Add-in another $5,000 month for HOA dues, rent, taxes and utilities and that's a total of $72,000 a month all-in for 50 Cent's three homes in Connecticut, New Jersey (rental), and Georgia (paid-in-full), but the majority went towards the Tyson Mansion.

In addition to the $72,000 per month, we also have to add-in the following expenses:

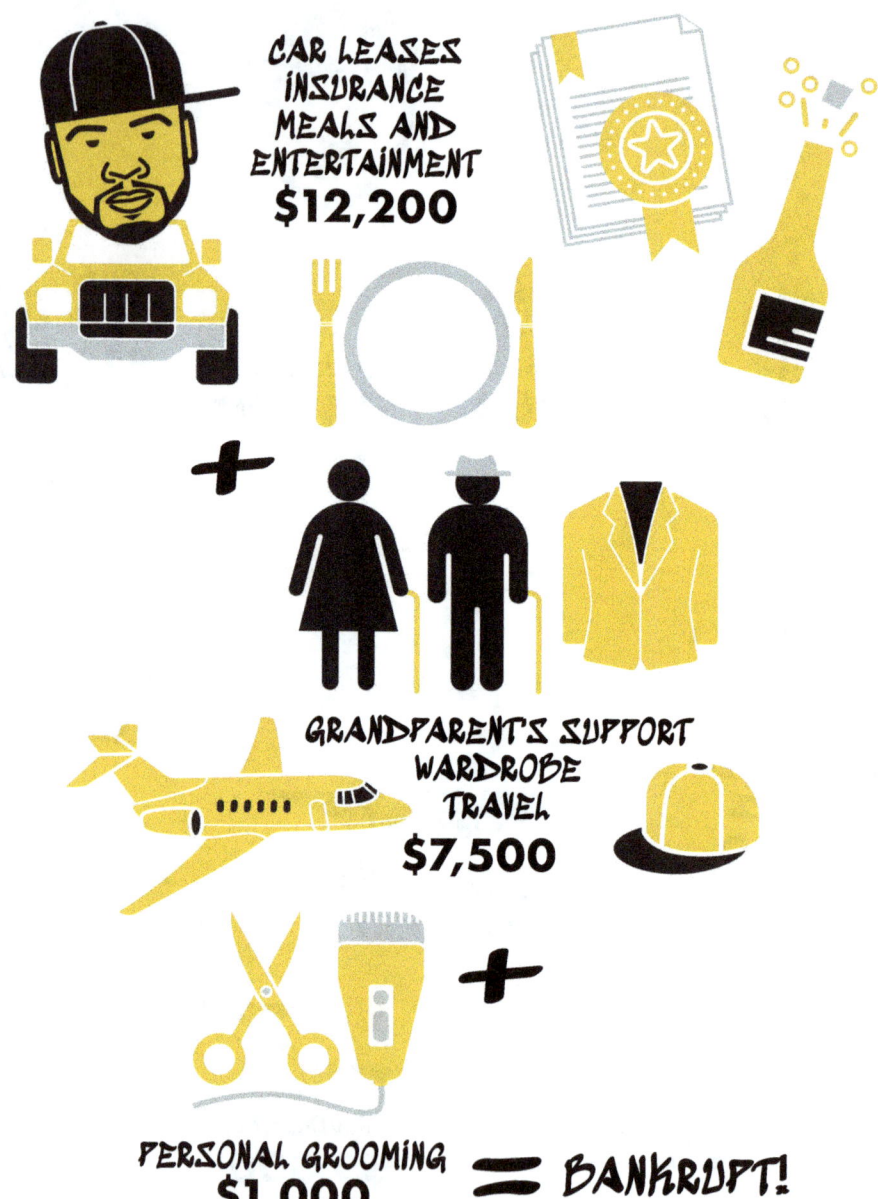

CAR LEASES
INSURANCE
MEALS AND
ENTERTAINMENT
$12,200

+

GRANDPARENT'S SUPPORT
WARDROBE
TRAVEL
$7,500

+

PERSONAL GROOMING
$1,000
= BANKRUPT!

A few quick CFP® notes:
• "Telephone" at $600 per month is perhaps the only thing remotely close to a 'normal person's budget.

• How can you spend more per month on your "wardrobe" than taking care of your grandparents who lost a daughter and took you in at *age eight*?

• "Child Support". Sing the hook with me again: I'm not saying she's a gold digger, but she ain't messing with no broke-broke...

• Seven cars for one person isn't smart. Leasing depreciating assets is though. I really thought "Meals and Entertainment" and "Travel" would be a lot higher.

All in, 50 had claimed his monthly expenses total to about $108,000, or about just $1.3 million a year. Speaking to *The Guardian* in 2020, his reasoning for filing was that,

"...it let him start over fresh," and that,

"...businesspeople will do that in a heartbeat before losing money. Because it means they have the ability to be secure and invest again."

What is a small wonder though, and 50 being a businessman, is that he didn't file for bankruptcy sooner to avoid "losing money", "start fresh", and "secure and invest again".

MAKING BETTER DECISIONS PAYS

Only 50 and his lawyers know the real story, but it is probably not a coincidence that he filed for bankruptcy after losing his lawsuit to Rick Ross's ex-girlfriend and before he landed his Starz deal. At any rate, he became debt-free in 2017, after successful ventures with said Starz deal (a reported $150 million), Effen Vodka (a reported $60 millionC), and writing a self-help book for aspiring hustlers in 2020 aptly named, Hustle Harder, Hustle Smarter. As of that COVID book release, he was sheltering-in-place in a new 3-story apartment in NYC, and more recently, went back out for his "The Final Lap Tour" becoming only the 4th hip-hop tour grossing more than $100 million. He had turned his life around. Making better decisions professionally and personally will do that for you.

HOW TO BUDGET LIKE A CFP®

After that read, do you still want to own a home? You may hate paying rent every month and feel like you're throwing away your dollars, but it's the most you will pay each month. A mortgage is the least amount you will pay each month. Trust me from personal experience.

You have to make sure your math works and then leave some wiggle room every month for surprises because they will happen. Hence the advice: some things in life you should buy (appreciating assets like an affordable home) and some things you should lease (rent; a mansion, a Ferrari, and/or a yacht.) The sheer upkeep costs on these luxury items make the deck stacked against you for any worthwhile appreciation unless you rent out the mansion and yacht and keep the Ferrari in mint condition.

Chances are not likely that you, nor I, are going to rent those luxury items like 50 and other high-income earners buy. Chances are nearly 100% that we all just want food on the table, a place to call home, and the ability to treat ourselves to modern conveniences, take a vacation(s), and spend time with loved ones. But how?

Simple. You only have to write down what's coming in after taxes, and what's going out.
I've been using detailed budget sheets for 20+ years with my clients. I can see the dread on their faces when I slide it across the table to

Sample:	
$5,000	Net Inflows
- $4,000	All Outflows
= $1,000	Your Cashflow

them or ask if they got it finished for me. I'm really not sure why—because they know they're overspending? It's always funny to me that if you know you have a problem or something to work on, why wouldn't you just strap your Nike's on and just do it?

Here are the only instructions.

1. Round down your after-tax income, and
2. Round up your expenses.

It's all about capturing your best, most realistic cashflow number each month. Secondarily, if you're underwater and barely getting by, or just plain pissing away money every month, we use your numbers as a way to prioritize what's most important to you.

– THE 50-25-25 RULE –

Keep in check by following this advice. Live off 50%, save 25%, and be able to pay up to 25% in total taxes. If you want Starbucks every day, no problem if it fits in your 50% and you can still save 25%. However, if you're short $80-$100 per month and have nothing else you can cut back on, you're going to need to at least cut down on your daily trips, or better yet, brew good coffee at home (my preference and cheaper).

Let's say you do the work and follow the 50-25-25 rule: write down your budget, get your priorities right about what's most important to you, cut all other needless subscriptions/wants, and save up every month for a downpayment on an affordable house.

Here's a "not-so-secret", secret that banks use to see if you can afford that home: a bank will loan you up to 28% of your gross income (before taxes) for a mortgage. If you make $100,000 a year, then you can afford a monthly payment of around $2,300. Now, you can choose to put down 20% of your affordable homes price as a down payment to not have to pay something called "PMI" (or professional mortgage insurance). To be honest though, my wife and I did not have the 20% to put down, but we did have 10%.

Guess what? I was terrified by the largest

purchase in my life thus far and wanted to keep extra cash back for all of the horror stories I had heard from clients (AC unit, water heater, new windows, roof…). Through appreciation, our house rose in value enough in 2-3 years to drop that PMI. The surprise we had from our lender was that they required 25% loan-to-value, meaning our home had to go up in value by 15% from when we bought it. When it was re-appraised (that's when the bank comes out and says what's it "worth"), we were shitting bricks. 25.25% Not even lying.

Guess what else appreciates with your home value? Real estate taxes and home insurance. Even when you pay off your mortgage 30 years later.

So, do you really ever own your home? Technically, what you do get is a chance to build equity—the difference between what you sell something for minus what you paid for it.

BIG PURCHASES

Big purchases, like 50's purchase of the Tyson Mansion, are the easiest way to mess up a perfectly great budget. I have a simple life rule before I make a big decision or a big purchase: I wait at least one week. Spontaneous purchases, nor well-researched decisions, usually come with buyer's remorse.

We have already gone over one of the biggest purchases in life; a home, but here are some other substantial purchases that can either set you back or forward depending on your cashflow choices.

HOW ABOUT A CAR?

Your first car may be a comped by your parents, but what about the first car you buy? Cars are depreciating assets (i.e. they go down in value once you drive them off the dealer's lot). Always buy used. My go-to is "gently broken in" at around 2-3 years old and 30,000+ miles on them. You should buy then if there is a major mechanical issue and a nice discount from new. As always mind your cash flow.

Tip: a bank will loan you up to 8% of your gross income. For example, if you make 100K, you can get a car loan up to $667 per month. But that doesn't mean you have to get a loan for up to that amount. Anything less than that, you save more cash flow to do something else, like invest.

HOW ABOUT COLLEGE?

Let's be honest, college was turned into a business a long time ago. Is it right for you or not? I've had so many clients show me some outrageous loan balances for higher education and it's just not paying off for them. The current US system is set up to put you in debt for 20 years. The government will not forgive your loans, that's a lie and an affront to the parents out there who worked two to three jobs to put their kids through college.

Do yourself a favor and watch Mike Rowe's Dirty Jobs. You don't have to go to college to make a good living for yourself. Right now, because of the amount of baby boomers retiring, there is a severe imbalance of trade jobs like electricians, welders, and plumbers. You can easily make six-figures a year without the noose of six-figure college debt. Consider all your options.

If you are considering college and the debt that comes with it, here's my rule: don't take on more debt than your first-year earnings of your profession. That means if you want to become a teacher making $50,000, don't run up college debt of $80,000. It's simply not sustainable when you graduate.

Instead, consider studying abroad in Europe. You'll have access to great schools that teach in English, with access to great travel and culturing experiences to boot. Your global network of friendships will multiply and provide you access to opportunities that your US friends won't have.

Already went to undergrad school and are considering grad school? Shop your options. There are a lot of options from employer-paid school or cost-effective online grad school. The cost of an MBA (Master of Business Administration) is around $50,000 in the US. The problem is, so many people went and got one, that's it's not worth the cost. For my profession of financial planning, it made more sense for me to get an industry- specific CERTIFIED FINANCIAL PLANNER® designation for around $10,000 online. My online school was after work each day, but beyond convenient at a great price. Your education should be specific to your profession- it'll help you go way farther and make more money... for more cash flow.

HOW ABOUT TRAVELING?

Almost everyone would like to travel but finds it an extra expense out-of-touch. I know, I did it before I got my cash flow correct. Unless you have parents that footed the bill for you.

When I was in college, I always had to stay back and work while others got to go on "spring break". I needed money, my parents weren't going to pay to let me party in Florida for a week, and guess what? I'm thankful for that. I saved up as much as I could, and instead, went West on winter break with the ski club for relatively cheap. I got to experience mountain life and make new friends and memories. While we did party, I at least got some exercise. That's what I tell myself at least.

After college though, I was a broke joke accumulating more debt just trying to make it from month to month, so I didn't go on a vacation for years. Like five years. I couldn't even afford to go out with my friends because I couldn't justify literally pissing credit card debt down the urinal. It was a hopeless and lonely time, but it let me dream about a future when I could travel.

When I met my wife, I was in a much different financial situation and was ready to make up for the lost time by "revenge adventuring". My first of three trips to Europe in a year was flying into Venice, Italy, taking the train up to Zurich, Switzerland, driving to Berlin with my future in-laws on the Autobahn- a bucket list wish, and then flying into Israel for a week and a half- not on my bucket list because I don't tan. My point is that if you think you're behind, you can always catch up quickly. How about realizing it happens when it's supposed to for your cash flow, or when you have enough credit card points saved up?

What about the whole engagement and wedding cost lie?

Once you meet "the one", it's a truly exciting time to be alive. Sometimes Cupid works fast, or sometimes it takes even longer, or sometimes even not, but if you walk into a jeweler the standard response for a ring budget is three months of salary. What? If you make $5,000 a month, you're going to spend $15,000? That's a great start to a down deposit on a home or at least a few great vacations. Before the engagement process was turned into a societal guilt business, just like college, people got simple gold bands to symbolize their love. A diamond isn't going to make your marriage work. Good cash flow habits will though. Nearly 40% of all divorces are caused by bad money decisions, so buy something you can afford and realize you can always upgrade in the future when you can afford it.

"Nearly **40%** of all divorces are caused by bad money decisions."

Speaking of marriage, weddings may take the cake for the societal guilt business. Who's not getting shaken down for the average $30,000 bill? Both sets of parents are pushed to pay for the one-day circus, the bride and groom's friends go on ridiculous "last romp" bachelor and bachelorette trips, all guests attending (or not) are encouraged to send a gift, and of course, the bride and groom pick up any leftover tab. All for a "perfect day" where you hug everyone but spend no quality time with anyone. A picture book of everyone dressed up creating "memories". Is there a better way? It's up to you and your future spouse, but remember marriage is all about the "ever-after". If you're broke after the wedding or set unrealistic expectations, not a great start to your "ever after". Hence, why almost half of marriages end in divorce.

Want another idea? My wife and I decided to have a small destination wedding in Florence, Italy. The theme? Equally Inconvenient. With my wife and I being from two different cultures, we wanted a place where it was difficult for all to come to, where no one could speak the language, but where we all could break bread, eat pasta, and "cheers" to world-class Chianti. The result? It was small, spent quality time with our guests, and relatively cheap. We, of course, wished we had more family and friends in attendance, but we hosted a wedding party after we got back to share pictures, eat more pasta, and drink more wine.

You do you, but keep your mind on your cash flow and be creative. Thinking outside of the box is a good muscle to develop in the world of wealth.

"...each child costs you nearly **$250,000** in the first world"

LASTLY, KIDS?

I'll keep it simple. From personal experience, there is a world of difference in wanting to be a parent, versus actually being a parent. I also don't think there's a time when you'll be ready. There are sacrifices in having children younger or older or adopting. Some people choose to never have kids. Just do the best you can and understand from a financial point each child costs you nearly $250,000 in the first world. That's a ton of cash flow to prepare for, but somehow, someway it gets done. It'll also make you more focused even as you're simultaneously more sleep deprived. If you haven't had kids yet, that last line will make sense to you.

CASH FLOW AND THEN RESERVES

Final point: once you get your cash flow right and goals in order, always keep reserves. Life happens and it can happen fast. The basic financial advisor's advice is to keep three-to-six months of your expenses in cash.

For 50's $108,000 monthly budget, that would've been a gaudy $324,000 to $648,000. For MC Hammer's $500,000 monthly budget, that would've been $1.5 million to $3 million. It's easy to see why they both ended up in Chapter 11 personal bankruptcy court. Don't blow it like Hammer, 50, or even Mike Tyson. Have a budget, spend wisely, and keep reserves.

3-6 MONTHS!

Cue Macklemore's "Thrift Store":

> **"**I'm gonna pop some tags
> Only got 20 dollars in my pocket
> I'm, I'm, I'm hunting, looking for a come up
> This is f*cking awesome.**"**

TAKE ACTION!
BUDGET LIKE A CFP®

THE 50-25-25 RULE:
- LIVE OFF 50% NOW
- SAVE 25% FOR LATER
- PAY 25% IN TAXES

CASHFLOW AND RESERVES
- KNOW YOUR MONTHLY EXPENSES, AND
- ALWAYS KEEP THREE TO SIX MONTHS IN CASH. ALWAYS.

BIG PURCHASES
- IF YOU CAN'T BUY IT TWICE, YOU CAN'T AFFORD IT. SO RENT IT.

– END OF TRACK 4 –

TRACK 5.

SPEAKERS, NOT SNEAKERS

TRACK 5: SPEAKERS, NOT SNEAKERS

In track one, we learned about the debt row
and how to break the cycle.

In track two, we learned the importance
of building and maintaining credit.

In track three, we learned about how to make
money and the life of an entrepreneur.

In track four, we learned about cash flow and
the importance keeping a budget.

Now, in track five, we will learn how to invest. Let's go.

The largest single sale of a hip-hop product almost didn't happen. In
hindsight, there was no questioning Apple's $3 billion purchase price
of Beats by Dre in 2014, but rather the genesis of the product idea. It
was not a straight line from start to finish. This is an investing story
from idea to product to sale; one that only came to fruition through
collaboration, money, time, and execution. My personal definition of
successful investing. Dr. Dre, the original producer and founder of
hardcore hip-hop, had created and mastered the entire genre from the
late 1980s well into the 2000s. The mastermind producer behind the
seminal music of N.W.A., his solo albums The Chronic and 2001, and
then discovered, signed, featured, and produced icons: Snoop Dogg,
Eminem, 50 Cent, and Kendrick Lamar. That's the short hit list.

He had thrived and survived during N.W.A.'s break-up, co-founded
Death Row Records with the notorious gang boss Suge Knight, and
the 90's East Coast versus West Coast beef that saw the deaths of the
period's legends 2pac and Biggie. He then rose again from the ashes to
found Aftermath Records. His superpower was music, combining the

best rappers with his signature beats. There simply wasn't anything left to prove in the rap game.

Until… Napster happened. Before Napster, artists sold CDs and cassette tapes all to go platinum. Internet streaming, playlists, shuffling, or suggested artists based on taste were years away. When Napster arrived, it put the entire industry in a death spiral. Music was being digitally copied for free and shared via MP3, drying up any new sales revenue, and leaving only touring revenue for artists. The music industry was in a free fall for a few years until Apple's invention of a $400 iPod in late 2001, creating a playing device for your digital MP3s. Besides holding a respectable 1,000 songs and boasting a 10-hour battery life, it only came with a cheap, sub-standard $2 pair of earplugs. For artists like Dre whose life's work was making music that you could feel, this was the final slap in the face. He reportedly told Jimmy Iovine, "Man, it's one thing that people steal my music. It's another thing to destroy the feeling of what I've worked on."

Dre was one of countless frustrated artists at the time before the previously mentioned streaming platforms were created, new revenues came back in, and the hardware caught up to the software.

As the story is told, back in 2006, a major shoe brand approached him for a collaboration. There had been some previous hip-hop mogul successes in urban clothing and sportswear by both Sean John (P. Diddy) in 1998 and Rocawear (Jay-Z) in 1999, so Dre was intrigued. Instead of a collaboration, he was more interested in his own line— true to his entrepreneurship style that lifted him from the streets of Compton to sitting atop the hip-hop producer world. Selling branded shoes to his millions of fans worldwide made sense, but something didn't feel quite right. Looking for guidance from another industry titan, he turned to Interscope Record Executive Jimmy Iovine. The now-classic line Jimmy said to Dre was focusing on what they both knew:

"F*ck sneakers, let's sell speakers!"

The power of their creative partnership created the right idea. Like most rappers needing his producing genius to make hit records, Dre needed Jimmy's genius advice to focus on a product answer for their music problem. Dre's genius was asking for advice when he was unsure. Hindsight is always 20/20, but I don't think you or I will ever regret getting a second opinion on anything in life.

Remember that lesson and this one too: when investing, stick with what you understand. You may think you're missing an opportunity, but it's better to pass and do what you do best. There's a lot of power in the word "no", so you can say "yes" to the right opportunity. The sneaker line that never happened may have done just as well or better than Kanye's Yeezys, but it didn't solve the problem that mattered most to them. By staying true to their instincts and knowledge, they knew what to do next with their investments of time and money.

Product research: create a product and get feedback from reliable sources. Why waste your time and money if it doesn't resonate? Especially in a new product. You must spend your capital wisely when investing; try to minimize your risks as much as possible and maximize your rewards. Stating the obvious, both of them were rich men before this idea, so they could afford to risk some money in order to make some money. [3]They never put all of their assets into this one, new venture, they only diversified their wealth. [4]That's called asset allocation, the act of not putting all of your eggs into one basket.

Dre and Jimmy next created prototype speakers and headphones. Noticeably with more bass to feel those beats. Using their vast network of artists across all genres they began offering up impromptu listening sessions to none other than 50 Cent's monster-anthem and Dre-produced hit "In Da Club". Jimmy had all kinds of artists coming in and out of Interscope to listen and give valuable input, input directly from the musical source, not sound engineers. Who better to give opinions? Artists like: M.I.A., Pharrell Williams, Gwen Stefani, and will.i.am all provided that input, and more importantly, felt ownership

[3] *There is no guarantee that a diversified portfolio will enhance overall returns or outperform a non-diversified portfolio. Diversification does not protect against market risk.*
[4] *Asset allocation does not ensure a profit or protect against a loss.*

in the creative process. It was the FUBU philosophy (For us, by us) that eventually got the famous musicians repping the headgear and their fans wanting to be like them and buying. Genius product launch.

To give credit where credit is due, it was will.i.am's idea to encourage Jimmy Iovine to pursue hardware before Jimmy floated the idea to Dre. To which Jimmy said,

"You know why they call it hardware? Because it's hard!"

The idea won out though, and will.i.am was an original investor who was handsomely rewarded. How much? No one knows, but he used the sum to fund his i.am.angel foundation, whose mission is to "administer charitable activities and programs targeted towards providing college scholarships (i.am scholarship), college preparation (i.am College Track), and opportunities in STEAM education (Science, Technology, Engineering, Arts and Mathematics)."

Lesson: if your investments pay off, you can choose to make a difference and pay it forward. Or as the Jay-Z line from "Moment of Clarity" goes:

> **"I can't help the poor if I'm one of them.
> So, I got rich and gave back, to me that's the win-win."**

Get yourself in a position to help and then don't forget to help.

In 2008, when Beats by Dre headphones were introduced, the marketing centered around "hear what the artists hear" with that intentionally bass-heavy sound. They weren't designed for classical music; they were for modern music like 50, Beyoncé, Kanye, Rihanna, and Drake. With Dre's well-respected name attached to every pair as well as other heavyweights like P. Diddy-branded "Diddybeats" and Lady Gaga-branded "Heartbeats", in addition to product placement in videos, Beats by Dre headphones became a cultural fashion statement. The product, and the answer to their music problem, went viral and profits soared along with their net worths.

Tapping into celebrity musicians launched the brand, but adding sports allowed it to expand. Superstars like LeBron James and Serena Williams were both brought into the fold as brand ambassadors to permeate the sports world. Just like 50 Cent's equity deal with Vitamin Water, James opted to take a small stake in the company for his endorsement. Another way to invest— lend your image or likeness in exchange for equity (stock or share of a company) now, with the chance of a payout later. Better put: invest your time now, for (hopefully) more money later. Sometimes equity and stocks become worthless. For LeBron though, he's thought to have made at least $30 million from his Beats by Dre endorsement stake when the company was sold to Apple in 2014 for a whopping $3 billion.

- KEEP SLIENT -

The original price offered was one more decimal, but a lot more money: $3.2 billion or $200 million more. Why the reduction in price? Someone couldn't keep their mouth shut until the ink was dry and checks were written. A piece of advice for anyone getting ready to sell their company to another company, honor your non-disclosure agreement (NDA) or at least stay quiet until the checks are deposited. In this case, the largest acquisition in Apple's history was leaked prematurely by Tyrese Gibson on his Facebook and YouTube accounts, where Dre declared himself the "first billionaire in hip-hop" and Gibson said the "Forbes list had changed". By the next morning, someone had made the effort to at least delete the video and photos, but the damage had been done. Twenty days, and presumably many apologies later, the deal was announced $200 million lighter. Nonetheless, it made Dre, Jimmy, will.i.am, LeBron, and private equity group, The Carlyle Group, hundreds of millions of stacked Benjamins.

All for creating a product for a problem. Supply and demand. Price versus value. The story of Beats by Dre is how investing works: the same duality that exists between an artist and a producer, a player and a coach, customers and businesses, or financial advisors and their clients. There is always money, or time, in exchange for each other—on both sides of the scrimmage. There are great ideas and bad mistakes all along the way, but always remember, it's time in the markets, not timing the markets. Learn the investing game and you can make money too- or buy you time. Perhaps even allow you to change lives through charitable giving.

INVESTING 101

Entertaining hip-hop investing stories of the rich and famous aside, let's talk about investing on a beginner level. You have to start somewhere to get somewhere else, and it will take a while. Then one day, by making good and repetitive choices, you can find yourself in a position of wealth. This is why the face of the $100 bill, Benjamin Franklin, said, "An investment in knowledge pays the best interest."

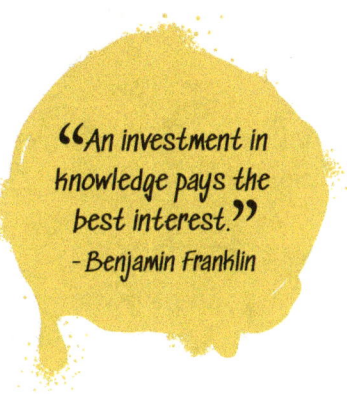

"An investment in knowledge pays the best interest."
- Benjamin Franklin

You have to learn before you earn. Why should you invest? Simple answer: to make your money work for you.

If you want to get out of bad debt like I did, invest the time needed to make a debt-free plan. If you want to prepare for the unexpected things in life, invest in an "Oh Sh*t" emergency cash account. If you don't want to work for the boss-man your entire life and retire, invest in retirement accounts and real estate. If you want to take vacations, enjoy life, and travel the world, invest so you can buy time off.

If you're thinking on a larger scale and want to solve a problem, like Dre did with Beats or Elon Musk has done with Tesla or SpaceX, invest in a new product.

If you want to give back and make a difference in the lives of the next generation, like Jay-Z and his "Book of HOV" at the Brooklyn Public Library or Andrew Carnegie's nearly 3,000 free public libraries across the English-speaking world, invest.

There are so many reasons to invest, except for not doing it. As

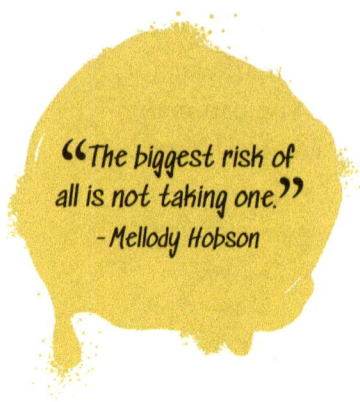

Mellody Hobson once said, "The biggest risk of all is not taking one." Just do it for your reasons, keep reasonable expectations, and be reasonable whether you win or lose. Good investing can lead to the financial freedom to make the best choices you see fit in your life. Not what anyone else is saying or doing, or what the business markets indicate, or what a government tells you to do. It's freedom from inflation, rent, or just getting by—the sky's the limit.

WHAT IS INVESTING?

Once you have your financial house in order and have leftover cash flow each month, you can begin to invest: The act of contributing something now and getting something greater back later.
As 2Pac rhymed in "Keep Ya' Head Up":

> "I'm tryin' to make a dollar out of fifteen cents,
> It's hard to stay legit and still pay your rent."

The general problem for most people is not getting money upfront and or staying patient, so many resort to get-rich-quick schemes or illegal means. This is not investing, this is desperation. What about gambling or playing the lottery? That's entertainment at best. As for running between the emotions of fear and greed, buying and selling with no plan in place. That's ignorance.

Investing requires patience and planning, an understanding of risk and reward, and the ability to keep an eye out today, as well as 10 years down the road. Most people need education on it, and if you don't have the time, then hire a financial advisor to teach you or to help manage your emotions. This is why I often refer to myself as a financial counselor and a professional hand-holder. Emotions can run strong on the rollercoaster ride of investing, so pick a ride that's comfortable for you. It's easy to make money on the way up ("keep it coming"), but heated on the way down ("I can't give enough reasons why to stay patient"). Master your emotions, ask for advice if you need it, and your investments will reap the rewards for you.

Think of the emotional rollercoaster ride Dre went on when Apple said, privately, that they'd buy Beats. They got excited and leaked the news online, which led to wondering if 20 days of apologies to other investors and Apple would result in the sale going through. It could've cost him way more than the $200 million had he kept his mouth shut and emotions in check. Easy to judge, but wisdom to share.

WHAT CAN YOU INVEST WITH?

You should invest with your head, your cash flow, and what OutKast said in "Hollywood Divorce":

> "*Promise Me You Gon' Stack,*
> *Promise Me You Gon' Ball,*
> *Promise Me You'll Invest Three-Fourths Of It All..*"

Is it possible to invest 75% of what you make? Probably not unless you strike gold or platinum status. However, the point is to make money, have fun while doing it, and always save to invest a substantial amount. Don't ever wonder how you're going to eat that month or likewise- just throw $25 in stocks, thinking it's going to add up to anything, and getting frustrated when it doesn't. It takes money to make money, so here's what to invest with:

CASH IS KING

If you've got cash stashed, then you can invest it right away. It buys everything, but cash alone doesn't grow. Low risk = low reward. Best put by Robert G. Allen, "How many millionaires do you know who have become wealthy by investing in savings accounts? I rest my case."

> "*How many millionaires do you know who have become wealthy by investing in savings accounts? I rest my case.*"
> -Robert G. Allen

If you're wondering, the answer is nada,

zilch, zero. Cash purchases everything around you. Paper or digital, it can be put to work, rather than sitting in a bank account doing nothing for you and earning double-digit interest for the bank. When you deposit $100 at the bank, do you really think they sit on it? No. They turn around and invest it by loaning out $90 of your money to someone else, allowing them to make that interest. Think like a bank- here's how.

GOOD DEBT

If you have left over, monthly cash flow and a good credit score, then you can get a loan from the bank to buy an appreciating asset. For instance, a rental property that can pay you back by making income every month. Using those freed-up dollars every month to pay the fixed loan back in smaller chunks allows you time for the asset to go up in value.

This is called good debt. Good debt provides several investing benefits.

Good debt buys you appreciating assets now.
Time lets them go up in value.

Good debt is a fixed cost; it stays the exact same.

Good debt is not taxed. Your income is.

Good debt gets you tax breaks.
Use these to lower your taxable income.

INFORMATION

Information is the most valuable asset to invest in. You can't see it or hold it like money, but the tiniest amount of it can have the largest impact on successful investing. It doesn't cost you anything to spend, but you have to acquire it first to be re-invested in later, just like Ben Franklin's quote. Or when will.i.am suggested "hardware" to Jimmy Iovine, and then Jimmy told Dre, "Speakers, not sneakers." Lack of information can humble you, whereas the use of it can multiply your efforts. Acquire it as your own asset to acquire more assets.

TIME

If you don't have cash, good debt, or information, there is one thing of equal value that everyone has everyday: time. It doesn't matter if you're broke or a billionaire, everyone has the same 24 hours in a day, seven days a week, and 365 days a year. Until you don't, it must be spent wisely.

Time is the most underrated currency, second only to information, with cash and debt lagging both by a mile. Just by showing up to work on time shows your reliability, interning for free to gain information, volunteering for a good cause to give back, and making time for family and friends to create lasting bonds- you can invest your time to give you a return on investment greater than any amount of money or good debt can purchase.

Reliability can get you a series of promotions and set you apart from the crowd. Gaining information creates the opportunity to use it to your advantage. Giving back shows others you genuinely care for your community. Creating lasting bonds will provide a group of people who are there for you, no matter what life throws at you in times of need.

Your time can also be traded for equity or a piece of a company. It's commonplace in start-up companies to give employees stock that can be sold later to compensate them for their time now if the company gets privately bought or sold on Wall Street. Just like when 50 Cent with Vitamin Water and LeBron with Beats were contracted to be brand ambassadors, they opted to take stock in lieu of money.

They followed the Lil' Wayne line from "She Will":

"I tried to pay attention, but attention paid me."

In both cases, they worked out exceptionally well; but they both could have gone nowhere. Their influence on pop culture, combined with the time they committed to the products, helped to lower the risk of failure and maximize the rewards for all involved. All with their investment of time.

A COMBINATION OF ALL FOUR

You can become outright dangerous when you combine all four of these at your disposal to invest in. Knowing how to use each one to their fullest potential in investing will not only make you wealthy and achieve the goals you set out for, but also impact the lives of those you love around you.

WHAT IS AN INVESTMENT?

Now that you have a clear idea of what you can purchase an investment with, what is an investment?

An investment is something that can be purchased with the future goal that it will go up in value and/or create income for you. In order for your investment to make you money, you have to leave it be, choose to buy more, and/or sell when your desired goal has been met. An investment can be referred to as an "asset" and is all about increasing your "net worth" so you can create your own, independent wealth.

Kendrick Lamar spits this same knowledge in "YOLO":

> *"Invest In Your Future,*
> *Don't Dilute Your Finances,*
> *401k, Make Sure It's Low Risk,*
> *Then Get Some Real Estate,*
> *4.25% Thirty-Year Mortgage."*

Simply put: the purpose of investments is to make your money work for you and for businesses too. Businesses invest but with a few more zeros and commas than individuals. The purpose of any business is to make money, so it's only natural that they are ruthlessly efficient with their capital-making investments that provide growth, time, and human capital. Think: our story of Apple buying Beats. Apple acquired Beats because it created and dominated the headphone market. It would've taken Apple years to build their own headphones, if even successful. Remember many other headphone wannabes failed to create a similar successful headphone. The answer: Just write a check to buy them and their creative talent. No need to start from scratch. With

Apple's $150 billion pile of cash in 2014, the $3 billion check to acquire Beats was a whopping 2%. Almost a rounding error for them.

For my small business, I could always acquire another retiring advisor's business, but I grow for free from word-of-mouth from my existing clients. I use free lightly because I've worked hard for two decades to earn my client's trust and business. Instead, I invested in human capital and time. Investing in the right assistants has allowed me to focus on what I do best while letting them do the administrative tasks they do best. Investing in an office location a mere five-minute walk down the street, pays me back every day. That's an extra 40 minutes a day by not driving, or an extra 16 workdays a year. That's an investment I'll make every time.

In 2019, Canadian cargo line, Cargojet, decided to invest in a publicity stunt for the ages and "gifted" a Boeing 767 private jet to rapper Drake. The cost? $185 million to completely renovate the 23-year-old "Air Drake", and the catch? He has to post to his millions of followers on social media while in it. The company believes the social media exposure alone will pay for the cost of the overhaul and maintenance, but he reportedly picks up the tab for fill-ups. An ongoing win-win partnership for both sides. It's unclear if he actually "owns" the aircraft and actual contractual details are private, but at least he didn't buy a depreciating asset… no matter how pimped-out it is. Alas, not everyone can get Drake's private jet deal, so here's a list of personal investments and how to make them work for you.

SCHOOLS OF HARD KNOCKS

Just as we touched on how to invest your time, education is the greatest investment in yourself. If you want to invest in what you understand, you better start getting educated. It doesn't matter where you're at, there are libraries and schools, and that thing called the Internet. You are living in a time where there's never been more information available at your fingertips—and for free. So, you may not need an expensive undergrad, graduate, or doctorate degree. In the game of life, it's not how much you make, it's how much you owe and how much you can save.

TRADES

There are so many opportunities in the trades (think: plumber, electrician, welder, crane operator), you can make more than a college grad with a student-debt noose around their neck. Grab an apprenticeship, learn everything you can from an older master looking to retire, and take over.

CLASSES

Warren Buffet, the G.O.A.T. of investing, said his best investment ever was a public speaking course. Make yourself better and do what you're afraid of—that's how you grow and add tools to your tool kit. Take any online courses and classes offered for free or learn hands-on from…

INTERNSHIPS

I discovered my calling in life through a chance internship at Merrill Lynch and absorbed the culture and dreams of the finance industry. 50 Cent interned under Jesse Itzler to break into the music industry and grow his network of contacts. It's who you know, not what you know, and like Biggie said, "if you don't know, now you know."

LICENSES

Even if you drop out of school or get stuck with a worthless degree and a mountain of debt, you can regain focus and income by getting licenses and certifications. Real estate agents only need to graduate high school and pass the real estate licensing course. I wonder how much of a commission the real estate agent who sold Jay-Z and Beyoncé their $200 million Malibu mansion made? If the agent only charged 1% instead of the normal 6%, that's a cool $2 million for one sale. Study up!

CERTIFICATIONS

If you finish a degree and want to specialize, consider a certification. For me, I went for my CERTIFIED FINANCIAL PLANNER® certification in late 2019. I had the dumb luck of signing up for an accelerated online course before the pandemic shut down. Working full-time from home and going to school every night of the week sheltered me from any of the boredom that drove people crazy. I had planned on having no free time when everyone else was binge-watching shows. It added an immeasurable amount of knowledge and wealth to my bottom line. Knowledge always pays. Get paid!

READ

If all else fails, read books. Leaders are readers, but not all readers are leaders. Knowledge and perspective are dangerous weapons to wield. 2pac studied Shakespeare when he was attending the Baltimore School of Art and was an avid reader of books. Think that helped him in the rap game?

FDIC AND FREE

"Cash is King" for purchasing, but a standalone investment? It is not. There are only two notable exceptions backed by the FDIC, short for Federal Deposit Insurance Company, where the federal government will make you whole if your bank goes under.

1. FDIC-insured cash is free from investment risk and insured up to $250,000 per account. Not nearly the $100 million that boxing champ Floyd Mayweather shared in 2011 that he had in his checking account. If the bank goes under, you get a max of $250,000. Let's hope Floyd diversified his cash into 400 more accounts.

2. Certificates of Deposits (CDs) pay you a specific interest rate for a specific amount of time. Think: 5% for 12 months. Your money is locked up, so if you need it, you lose the interest. This is generally great for grandma and grandpa who prefer a return, but little to know no risk. Except for when interest rates go up or down, that is called interest rate risk. High Yield Savings Accounts (known as HYSA's) pay you a floating, but competitive interest rate for your liquid cash. Still FDIC-insured like CDs but with added access. Think: 4% on any sum of money. It can go up or down at any time, but you can take it

out at any time without losing interest. It pays a little less interest than a CD, but you have access to your cash when you want it, and it has a greater interest-rate risk than CDs. That's the safety trade to hide in, but if you're looking for real returns, here's where to look next.

WU-TANG FINANCIAL

Back in 2003, Chappelle's Show on Comedy Central was a hit. I used to watch every episode, laughing so hard I cried at Dave's comedy genius. It was so racially inappropriate, it'd leave you speechless: Tiger Woods and the Racial Draft, Charlie Murphy and Prince playing basketball (skins v. blouses). In another episode, Dave made the now-classic skit about "Wu-Tang Financial" where he, the RZA, and the GZA reference their hit "C.R.E.A.M." (Cash Rules Everything Around Me) and would devise the "best plan for your fam" to "diversify your bonds n***a" and "protect ya neck"! Because at the end of the day: "Wu-Tang Clan ain't nuthing ta f*ck wit."

Classic rhymes from classic times.

What Dave was making fun of was the pale, male, and stale-dominated world of the financial services industry. Investments, like stocks, bonds, mutual/index funds, and annuities, were and still are vague terms discussed by some, and understood by even less. [5]Long before ETF's (short for exchange traded funds), crypto currency, or meme stocks became a thing. Let's break it down by each so it's not a foreign language.

STOCKS

Stocks are a small piece of a company. Its value can go up and down (think: growth stock) or stay boring and pay a steady dividend. They can be bought in full shares or fractional shares; whatever fits your budget. They can go to the moon or fall to zero. Stocks allow for high risk but have rewarded investors with about 10% returns per year over the last 50 years.

---

[5]ETFs trade like stocks, are subject to investment risk, fluctuate in market value, and may trade at prices above or below the ETF's net asset value (NAV). Upon redemption, the value of fund shares may be worth more or less than their original cost. ETFs carry additional risks such as not being diversified, possible trading halts, and index tracking errors.

BONDS

[6]Bonds are the debt of a company. When you own a bond, the company pays you interest as if you were the bank collecting interest from your depositors. They are typically sold in blocks of $1,000 for company debt or $100 for government debt. They generally carry less risk and can also go to zero, but if a company goes under, you get paid before the stockholders. Bonds have paid out a long-term average of around 5% per year or about half of stocks. Generally, when stocks are down, bonds are up.

Whether it's stocks or bonds, it's all about balance, baby. The best mix is to hold many stocks and bonds and/or a blend of both. But how? Easy. Buy a simple mutual fund or index fund.

MF'S AND IF'S

[7]Mutual funds and index funds are automatic diversification that spreads-out your investment risk. They reduce single stock or single bond risk by owning lots of different companies' stocks and/or bonds. Mutual funds generally hold about 100 stocks whereas Index funds own an entire index. [8]Think S&P 500 = 500 largest US stocks. The founder of Vanguard Funds, John Vogle, said it best,

> **"Don't worry about the needle in the haystack, buy the haystack."**
> -John Vogle

"Don't worry about the needle in the haystack, buy the haystack." That's OG advice. John's strategy of owning the haystack led to the creation of one of the largest mutual and index funds companies in the world: Vanguard Funds. As of September 30th, 2024, Vanguard manages around $9.3 trillion. To put that into context, that's about 3,360 Jay-Z's. That's a lot of haystacks.

---

[6]*Bonds are subject to market and interest rate risk if sold prior to maturity. Bond values will decline as interest rates rise and bonds are subject to availability and change in price.*

[7]*Investing in mutual funds involves risk, including possible loss of principal. Fund value will fluctuate with market conditions and it may not achieve its investment objective.*

[8]*The S&P 500 is a stock market index tracking the stock performance of 500 of the largest companies listed on stock exchanges in the United States. Indexes are unmanaged and cannot be invested in directly.*

ANNUITIES

[9]Annuities are pseudo-investments issued by insurance companies, not investment companies. Think of it as income: You take a lump sum amount of cash now, and the insurance company promises to pay a certain amount back to you every month for the rest of your life, with a small interest rate. Outlive how long they think you'll live and win out. Die younger, thank you very much for your contributions. Any pensions are annuities. Social Security is a federal annuity. Get it? Got it? Good. Now for the exciting stuff: real assets.

HOTLINE BLING

Let's talk about investing in what you can see and hold. Drive and live in. These investments are called real assets because they are just that—real—with real returns and not just a piece of paper.

ICE, CHAINS, ROLLYS & GRILLS

From the early 80s, rappers started donning extravagant jewelry. What started as thick gold chains, morphed into million-dollar custom, gold chains and platinum grills encrusted in diamonds. Rolexes and rings hung off the rapper's wrists and fingers. These are so custom, they're artifacts, and the market for resale is very exclusive. Highly illiquid, but if you have the net worth, cash flow, and want a family heirloom to pass down, be my guest. Chances are it'll fetch less than what you paid but look at King Tut. Priceless.

KICKS & JERSEYS

Anything sports-related: Jordans, LeBrons, and Nike collections. Hip-hop culture became fascinated with NBA-branded sneakers and jerseys of Jordan and LeBron. The newest editions that drop each year become the newest styles. There are special edition jerseys and kicks for everything now: all-star games, play-offs, finals jerseys; not just "home" and "away" versions.

Collectibles and autographed memorabilia have become big business

---

[9]*Fixed and Variable annuities are suitable for long-term investing, such as retirement investing. Gains from tax-deferred investments are taxable as ordinary income upon withdrawal. Guarantees are based on the claims paying ability of the issuing company. Withdrawals made prior to age 59 ½ are subject to a 10% IRS penalty tax and surrender charges may apply. Variable annuities are subject to market risk and may lose value.*

and good, long-term investments. Just like playing cards and comic books, they are graded by how perfect they are, so protect and never use them if you want to be able to attract the highest bidders from other collectors. Just remember, these are illiquid investments-meaning hard to turn into cash.

WHIPS

From the hydraulics and booming sound systems displayed in the 90's West Coast rap videos and then on MTV's Pimp My Ride, rapper's souped-up cars showed out and showed off. Good investment or bad? Depends on how much it costs, the upkeep, and the storage.

The rule of thumb is to lease (rent) depreciating (go down in value), over-the-top assets that go vroom and boom. Don't buy a Rolls Royce Phantom or Lamborghini Murcielago when you want to show off; rent it and return it. Unless you can truly afford it, which Jay-Z said you'd have to be able to "buy it twice." Simple formula from a billionaire.

CRIBS

When investing, Mark Twain shared this advice, "Buy real estate, they're not making it anymore." Sage advice from someone almost 200 years ago. Nothing has changed, except for the value of land and houses. Both went up substantially with relatively brief periods down (like 2007-2009); nonetheless, great investments if your net worth and long-term cash flow can afford them. When 50 Cent was showing off the Tyson Mansion on MTV Cribs, he was too busy living the high life to understand what happens when the lean times come.

> "Buy real estate, they're not making it anymore."
> - Mark Twain

Real estate is an appreciating asset, meaning its value goes up over time. So, on the surface, it's a no-brainer to invest in. You can get good debt or a fixed loan, at a fixed interest rate, and for a fixed term. The price may go up and down and back up again, but the debt only goes lower. As it goes up in value, you earn equity meaning positive value. What if it goes down? You already know if you have a car loan.

Depreciating assets like the cars you drive go down in value faster than you pay them off, meaning you get negative equity or lose value—same for the housing market at times. Real Estate is great, but:

1. You have to make sure you have the cash flow and pay the mortgage every month.
2. You plan to own it for the long term (ie. 10+ years) because they are illiquid and difficult to turn into cash fast.
3. You don't buy "high" or "overpriced" because you will be in a temporary hole. If you are forced to sell, you lose twice. Once on the short-term loss, and the other from the long-term gain you'll never see.

BONUS

If your bravado matches your bank account, you can run this town like the price paid by Mr. and Mrs. Sean Carter (Jay-Z and Beyoncé) in 2023 for the current California sales record. How much? A whopping $190 million mansion in Malibu which reportedly was a "deal" because it was originally on sale for $300 million. The high-net-worth class operates in longer zeros and commas, but a 30% discount is still a 30% discount. Unless it's over-priced, then you have a BIG problem of negative equity, right? Wrong.

They paid all in cash. That's right, they paid all $190 million, in cash, all at once, on one home. There is no loan or negative equity on the books, only a paid-up asset to borrow against if they choose to. Going on a hunch, but they plan on holding this real estate for a while.

WHAT'S THE 411?

With the four currencies we discussed at the beginning, let's skip both time and information and focus on cash. Cash can be both earned and loaned. It's using the money you have in the bank and using everyone else's money in the bank. You also need some guidelines on whether to buy, loan, or rent (BLR) certain investments. The who, what, when, when, and where. Good thing our friends at Wu-Tang Financial provided a 411 chart that you can check out in the ebook or book-book.

– END OF TRACK 5 –

WU-TANG FINANCIAL — PROTECT YO' NET WORTH

	BUY	OWN	RENT
💵 $ IS 👑	EVERYONE / ESRB	STACK YOUR CASH	USE CASH TO RENT
📈 ₿	EVERYONE / ESRB	YES! INVEST!	=ACTIVE TRADING G.L!
💎 ⛓ ⌚	RICH AND FAMOUS? YES!	IS IT AN INVESTMENT?	DON'T SPEND TO PRETEND
👟 23	EVERYONE / ESRB	IS IT AN INVESTMENT?	DON'T SPEND TO PRETEND
🚗	RICH AND FAMOUS? YES!	GET A LOAN IF PRACTICAL	NOT PRACTICAL? LEASE
🛥 🏠	RICH AND FAMOUS? YES!	LOAN + IS TAX-DEDUCT?	NOT PRACTICAL? LEASE
🚁 ✈️	RICH AND FAMOUS? YES!	LOAN + IS TAX-DEDUCT?	BEST WAY? AIR DRAKE

TRACK 6.

BACK YO' ASSETS UP!

TRACK 6: BACK YO' ASSETS UP!

If you've "started from the bottom and now you're here" in your financial journey, you're ready for wisdom that affects not you, but those who you love and came up with.

You escaped Debt Row.

You started making good credit decisions.

You became an entrepreneurial hustler baby.

You made steady cash flow and not "Mo' Money, Mo' Problems."

You made smart investments like Dre's Speakers, instead of Sneakers.

Now you're going to learn how to "Back Yo' Assets Up."

CASHFLOW & SAVINGS

Earlier on, we discussed getting your money right and having leftover cash every month. The next was needing to stack that cash for the lean times that will come no matter how high your star flies. The generic CFP® advice is three-to-six months of your expenses, so if you need $5,000 a month, that's $15,000 to $30,000. Keep that cash in a HYSA; short for: high-yield savings account. One where it's kept safe in an FDIC-insured savings account that pays you the highest, floating interest rate.

You're prepared, safe, and more secure… right?

Nope! One more huge detail. Whose name is on your cash accounts and investments? Did you set up a beneficiary or update it when life changed? Did your bank or investment representative even ask? Most do, but a lot don't. Let's tighten up.

TITLE-ING INSTEAD OF IDLING

If you answered, "The accounts are in my name, son", then great, until something unexpected happens like death or becoming incapacitated (ie: a coma; where you're alive, but unresponsive). When this happens, the goal should be to pass as close to 100% of what you made to those who you want to carry it forward after you die.

Which accounts? All bank accounts and any non-retirement investment accounts; like the ones you can open at Robinhood.

How should you title these? If you have a bank account or non-retirement investment account, you can have it "named" (that's registered or titled) in your solo name, or jointly when there are two or more people (for example married or with a parent/child). You do this when you open it, or you can always add it later. Because these accounts are not retirement accounts, you can add any of the following titling requests.

POD?
TOD?
JTWROS?

• A "POD" or "Payable On Death" designation (specifically at a bank),

• A "TOD" or "Transfer On Death" (specifically for non-retirement investment accounts), or

• "JTWROS" short for "Joint With Rights Of Survivorship" on any accounts.

Why do this? Because adding these titling features will keep your money made out of probate court and passed directly to whom you want to take care of and/or decide to leave your assets to. Not in the hands of exes, not distant 4th-cousins, not the kid from Michael Jackson's "Billie Jean", and definitely not any Kanye's "Gold diggers".

PROTECT YO' NECK

It's not enough that just your cash is insured by the FDIC. You need to be insured. Death and taxes are the only guarantees to us all, but do you know what escapes both? Answer: life insurance. How?

Death makes life insurance real, and in the US, life insurance pays out tax-free. That's a win-win—except when your name is on the policy that pays out. Which is exactly why the rapper French Montana spoke out in 2022 against record labels taking out life insurance policies on their artists . According to him, the rising death toll of young rappers prompted labels to insure their investments against their risk of loss. From his point of view, he sees them as profiting from an artist's death. But, in reality, they invest a lot of time, capital, and marketing to develop artists, and if an artist passes unexpectedly, they stand to lose—not to gain. The labels may be paid out millions and a temporary bump in posthumous sales (like in the cases of Biggie and 2Pac), but you're not getting your time back or future material from the artist.

TERM OR PERM?

[11]TYPES OF LIFE INSURANCE

There are many different types of life insurance, but it boils down to just two: Term and Perm. What's the difference? It's all in the name.

Term Insurance provides a specific amount of insurance (or coverage), for a specific time period (or term), and for a specific premium (or cost). Think: $1,000,000 for 20 years and $100 per month. It's the cheapest option for coverage, so it can save you dollars every month to be used elsewhere or for investing. In case of death, it's used to pay off mortgages and other debts, replace lost income, and/or fund education and expenses for any surviving children during the period. When year "21 Savage" comes around though, and your term expires, it becomes insanely expensive, so you can only afford to cancel. The goal here is "protect ya' neck" only as long as you need to and not anymore after that.

Perm Insurance (short for "permanent") does just what it says- it's designed to last your whole life. Just like term insurance, it provides a specific amount of insurance and for a specific price. However, you can design these to be paid up by having enough cash in it to pay the premiums till your death. How do you get that much cash built up? Because you have to put in extra per month, making this the most expensive type of insurance. The amount of coverage can be for the same reasons as term insurance or designed to leave tax-free money at your advanced-age death. [12]Speaking of old age, you can also add different riders (or options) to suit your needs. For example: a long-term care coverage rider where it pays someone to take care of you when you can't anymore.

Special edition remix trick: You can loan yourself the money that is accumulated inside your policy and not pay it back. It's all tax-free and doesn't affect your credit score. If you owe at death, it's just subtracted from the total life insurance payout.

The 411? What happens if you don't pay your premiums on your insurance? You're sent a nastygram letter gently reminding you to pay or your policy will "lapse". That's insurance slang for "canceled". Pay the premium or else. Insurance companies are gangstas.

BUY-SELL AGREEMENTS

The general purpose of life insurance is to protect against the risk of loss, but it can also help to make sure that businesses keep their doors open and protect employees' jobs. If you're a successful entrepreneur with employees, you need to consider what happens if you die. The answer: A mess and your business will cease to exist. How to protect

---

like personal advice you should consult an insurance professional. You may also visit your state's insurance department for more information.

[12]*Riders are additional guarantee options that are available to an annuity or life insurance contract holder. While some riders are part of an existing contract, many others may carry additional fees, charges and restrictions, and the policy holder should review their contract carefully before purchasing. Guarantees are based on the claims paying ability of the issuing insurance company.*

against this? Get a Buy-Sell Agreement on the books.

If you have a homie in the same business with the same problem, you can get a life insurance policy on each other to pay out to your family or estate to outright purchase your business. This makes the unknown known and gets a plan in place in case of your early departure. It won't be your problem, but it's the least you can do for the people who count on you- family, clients, and employees.

This is why I've set one up for my small business with my good friend who started in the same bullpen as me in 2003. A bullpen is the financial services version of a smiling and dialing call center where you become numb to rejection. Both of us started at the bottom, now we're here. We've worked too hard for over two decades to get where we're at, and want to make sure that our families, employees, and clients have a back-up plan just in case. Like all insurances, you only need them when you need them.

TRUST YOUR FAMILY?

Ever wonder where Jay-Z got the name Rockafella from? It's a play on the last name of one of the most ruthlessly successful robber barons of the Gilded Age; USA circa 1870s to 1900. Who was this man? John D. Rockefeller. He single-handedly turned his company, Standard Oil, into a US monopoly with 90% of the oil industry, by taking out his competition by any means. He absorbed and consolidated all other oil companies until he was the last man standing. When another robber baron, Frederick Vanderbilt of the railroad empire, tried to jack up his shipping costs, Rockefeller pivoted and invented pipelines to transport his oil everywhere, cheaper. The railroad industry all but collapsed afterward, but John D. became so powerful that the Supreme Court broke up his company into 34 separate companies in 1911.

So what does life insurance have to do with the real Rockefellers?

Another use for life insurance is to fund and refund a family trust. John D.'s family irrevocable trusts and family constitution were designed for creating and perpetuating generational wealth, which keeps the family rich, in theory, forever.

As opposed to the Vanderbilt family heirs who blew $2.3 billion; that's inflation-adjusted for what $100 million in 1877 is worth now. The estate was dwindled it down to only $1.5 million at the time of Gloria Vanderbilt's death in 2019. I guess Gloria's son, Anderson Cooper of CNN, still needs to keep working.

Compare that with the Rockefeller family's two trusts that are alive and well supporting nearly 200 descendants now, with steady income for all and around $8.4 billion of assets to borrow against. How? Every family member has a life insurance policy on them. When they die, the bucket is filled back up for the next generation. All tax-free. You don't build an empire with stupidity! You have to make a plan.

CPA ALL DAY

Let's say you're a successful entrepreneur, doing what you love, and getting paid for it. Life is great and chances are you've been able to afford to offload some of the worst parts of being in business- the actual business part. Who wants to do payroll, hiring, firing, and possibly the worst job: paying the "the Feds" your share of taxes?

I certainly don't like to, and the reason I hired a great Certified Public Accountant (CPA) to make sure I'm paying only my fair share. I'm fine with that no matter the number, because if you're making money, you're going to pay taxes on it. What I wished someone would've told me early on in entrepreneurship is to save at least 30% of what you make, because everything is paid out 100% with no taxes  withheld in 1099 income. The first time you get a tax bill is a bad moment. One that should be remembered and immediately fixed using a pro or at the very least a software program. Paying hundreds to file your taxes could save you thousands. I'll take that trade every time, t hat way I can focus on what I do best and use another pro for everything else.

Normally in business, your "tax man" is your CPA (Certified Public Accountant). It can also be an "EA" (Enrolled Agent) or some other trusted bookkeeper without any designations. Designations or Certifications just means your professional passed the required tests. Whether they're any good or not at their job isn't tested. That's why it's always helpful to research your pro, get a referral, and do your homework. As the saying goes, "Do someone right and they'll tell 10 others, do someone wrong and they'll tell everyone to keep moving along."

If you're a touring rapper selling millions and performing for millions with a preference for strip clubs, blunts, and purple sizzurp, your mind isn't on your money or your money on your mind. Chances are, you're living moment-to-moment.

Back in 2011 and 2012, Lil' Wayne (real name: Dwayne Michael Carter) ended up in tax $14.2 million in back taxes, penalties, late fees, and interest. Tax court for tax liens, owing a grand total of liens happen when you owe the IRS, but you neglect to pay them. This results in the federal government "securing their interest in your property". If you further refuse to pay or do not make arrangements to pay, they'll just go ahead and seize your property in the amount owed to settle your debts. This is called a tax levy. Or you can just hire a pro to make sure you're in the clear every year.

Why did this happen to Lil' Wayne and so many others? Because his accountant, or lack thereof, did not file or pay his taxes correctly, reportedly for years, going back to 2002. Yikes. Talk about trusting the wrong people, or worse, intentionally trying to underreport your income. Fortunately for Weezy (Lil' Wayne), he had a friend come in for the tax assist, none other than Mr. Shawn Carter (same last name, but no relation). It had been kept hush-hush, but Jay-Z helped him pay off his tax bill and in 2017, his tax liens were released by the IRS. No details were given other than a shout-out of gratitude during one of Lil' Wayne's 2018 concerts.

The IRS always wins, no matter what your business is: legal or illegal.

Look up famed Chicago mobster, Al Capone. He got caught not for his illegal businesses, but for unpaid taxes owed. He famously said in court, "They can't collect legal taxes from illegal money." Wrong. In 1931, Capone was sentenced to 11 years in federal prison for federal income tax evasion.

Moral of the story? You need to take your taxes seriously, if not, the IRS will. Not everyone has an Uncle Shawn to swoop in and to help solve your tax problems. Vet your pros first, build your team, and keep them honest. There are about 6,900 pages in the US tax code and almost 75,000 pages if you include the Department of Treasury's official interpretations of said tax code. If you have the right people, the pages can be used as "tax coupons" to legally lower what you owe.

LEGAL ILLS

When you get something that people want like fame, money, and power, the haters gon' hate and can drag you to court. Your legal ills can lead to bigger bills.

2PAC

Beefs, middle-finger to the rules, and accusations will picture you rollin' to court-court like 2Pac. He was in and out of court and jail during his shortened dramatic career and ultimately paid the price when he was murdered. Lightning rods attract lightning.
Solution: Play the long game and keep your mind, and mouth, silenced on distractions.

LIL' WAYNE

One more time for the people in the back. If you owe $14+ million in back taxes like Lil' Wayne? You get a ticket to the tax court.
Solution: If you file correctly in the first place, this is an easy court to stay out of.

MC HAMMER & 50 CENT

Can't pay your mortgage and bills like our examples of Hammer or 50?

You're going to personal bankruptcy court. Solution: Mind your cash flow and maintain a budget.

All courts have a few things in common, mainly that you need legal representation, aka an attorney. This will cost you a lot of time and money you've worked so hard to make, hence the Lawyer's creed: "A man is innocent until he has been proven broke."

Only you- and perhaps your trusted friends and family- can check your behavior, but the goal should be to stay out of court and only pay attorneys for planned personal, business, and estate legal needs.

Why? Because you worked hard your entire life, created something of value, accumulated some assets, and then get planted. Do you want to see the fruits of your labor go to either your loved ones and/or a cause you support?

If you say no, that's completely OK because it's your stuff, and your wish to not plan ahead. It may cause unintended consequences and years of disputes and legal fees, but any untitled assets will be going, going, back, back, to...probate court.

PROBATE COURT

What's a probate court? Easy answer: A place to make sure your assets stay out of when you die. A probate court is a court that manages the legal process of distributing a person's assets after they die, known as probate. Probate courts are responsible for the following steps:

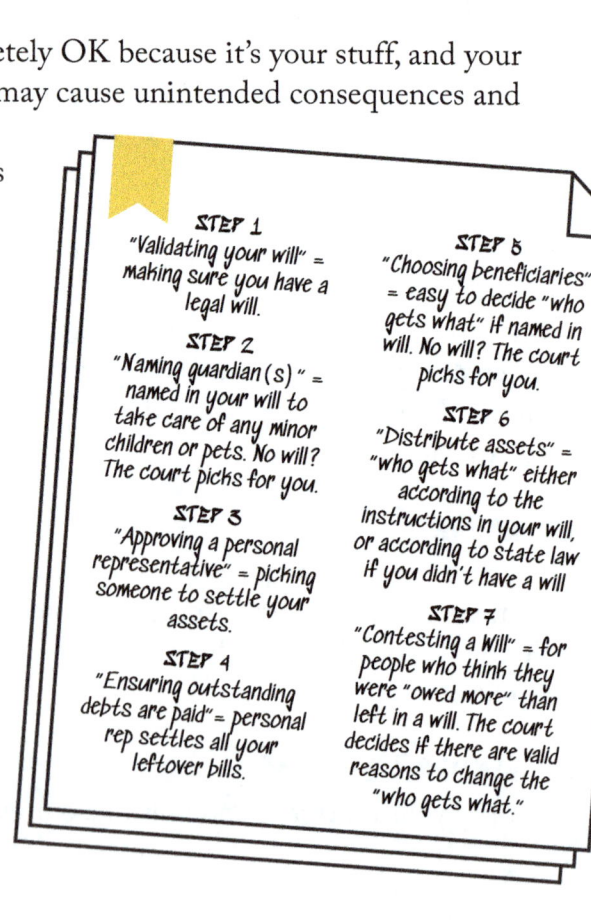

STEP 1
"Validating your will" = making sure you have a legal will.

STEP 2
"Naming guardian(s)" = named in your will to take care of any minor children or pets. No will? The court picks for you.

STEP 3
"Approving a personal representative" = picking someone to settle your assets.

STEP 4
"Ensuring outstanding debts are paid" = personal rep settles all your leftover bills.

STEP 5
"Choosing beneficiaries" = easy to decide "who gets what" if named in will. No will? The court picks for you.

STEP 6
"Distribute assets" = "who gets what" either according to the instructions in your will, or according to state law if you didn't have a will

STEP 7
"Contesting a Will" = for people who think they were "owed more" than left in a will. The court decides if there are valid reasons to change the "who gets what."

COST OF NOT PLANNING

How much does it cost in dollars? Probate can cost anywhere between 3% to 7%+ of the total estate value. How much does it cost in time? Probate can take up to one-to-two years. Probate court fees vary from state to state but can range from a few hundred dollars to over a thousand dollars for the certificate fee, filing fees, heir notifications, and document fees.

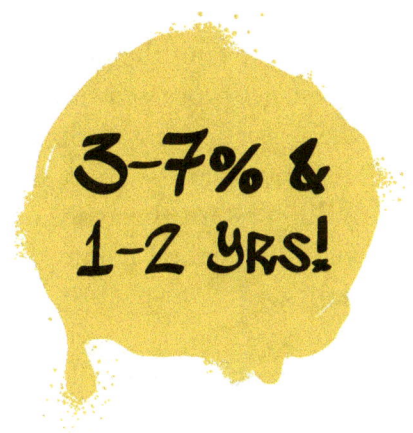

3-7% & 1-2 YRS!

When you have no will, that means you die "intestate" and the laws of the state that you reside in will decide the outcome.

TAKEOFF

When Takeoff from the rap group Migos, of "Bad and Boujee" fame, was shot and killed in a Houston bowling alley after a fight in late 2022, he died "intestate". Being only 28, with no wife or children, the last thing on his mind was having a will. He was at the top of the fame game and living his best life until it was tragically cut short. Life happens when you least expect it too.

For most people, getting married, having children, or getting a mortgage is a triggering event to get your legal needs right. Why? Because most people want their spouse and children to be taken care of—not having to go to court to keep your house or identify next of kin to become legal guardians for your kids. Even if you don't have a reported $28 million estate like Takeoff, you still need a will.

Since Takeoff was a Georgia resident, the State of Georgia Intestacy Laws applied. With no spouse or kids, the estate, once settled, will go to his next of kin- his surviving parents. The problem being that Takeoff's mother raised him without his estranged father, so he probably would've wanted his mother to inherit 100% of his assets. Since there was no will, now they are both fighting in court over his estate and whatever the State of Georgia decides will happen.

To understand the process, all of Takeoff's money, property, and other assets get processed through probate court. A personal representative is then assigned, any debts are paid off, and then the remaining assets are distributed as the court sees fit. If the total cost is 5% of his $28 million estate, then the court takes in $1.4 million. That doesn't even factor in Federal Estate (Death) Taxes up to 40% over applicable limits.

How much does a will cost? About $500-$1,000.

Dropping the mic here.

- DA' LEGAL HIT LIST -

 **TUPAC SHAKUR, 25** The rapper-actor was shot and killed in 1996 on the Vegas strip. Since he had no wife or children at his passing and having been a resident of the Golden State, California law directed his estate (worth about $200,000 at the time) 100% to his mother.

 **NATE DOGG, 41** When the "King of Hooks" died without a will in 2011, he left behind six children from different relationships, a wife, and one ex-wife. Probate outcome? After a 12-year legal battle, his estate settled with his widow and nine children for $2.7 million. The monies will be evenly distributed amongst his widow LaToya Calvin, and his original six children and bonus three discovered. Surprise!

 **PRINCE ROGERS NELSON, 57** After "The Artist Formerly Known as Prince" died in 2016 without a will or trust, his whopping $156 million estate was in probate court for six years. According to the Associated Press, after Prince died, "more than 45 people came forward as potential heirs to his estate, with many claiming to be a wife, child, sibling or other relative." One included an inmate who falsely claimed to be his son.

– BASIC LEGAL –

WILL-MATIC

Opposite Takeoff's situation was late-rapper Mac Miller. The "Self Care" artist must have received sound legal advice because he had set up a will and a living trust when he was only 21. He died of a drug overdose just five years later, but his parents, as the trustees of his trust, were able to handle his cash, assets, and real estate without going through probate court. This is just as legally intended to do in the event of an unexpected exit. A will makes your wishes simple and clean during an emotionally draining period for the loved ones you leave behind.

Since he passed away unmarried with no known children, by Minnesota law, his six siblings (full-blood sister and five half-siblings) inherited his estate. Why didn't he just spend a few thousand on a trust instead of paying $7.8 million in probate court fees? That's an expensive family soap opera.

 **BOB MARLEY, 36** The "Legend" reggae icon died in 1981, but on purpose without a will. Why? It was against his Rastafarian religious beliefs. It took over 30 years of contentious legal battles for his many family members and ex-lovers to settle his reported $30 million estate. Being a citizen of Jamaica, his country's intestacy laws were observed. Jamaican law gave 10% of his assets to his wife as well as another 45% of his estate. The remaining 45% was divided equally among his 11 kids. No estate plan, no cry?

 **JIMI HENDRIX, 27** The guitar legend died in 1970 without a will, spouse, or any known children. The legal fight over his estate alone took more than 30 years to resolve. The catch? His estate was only worth about $20,000 at death and had ballooned to about $80 million when his father inherited his son's fortune. When Jimi's father died in 2002, a new legal fight broke out between Jimi's siblings over the use of the late-guitar god's image. Finally, in 2015, a settlement was reached by all—only 45 years after his death. Don't have "Purple Haze"- get a will!

A will can solve this potential problem. The last thing you want to do is let the state execute your estate. Now you know, do something about it, and don't Takeoff without one. Be a real Mac.

TYPES

Wills can take many forms, before or after death, written or spoken, but there's a few main types: living, simple, and a testamentary trust. Each type is used for different purposes, so get the right legal docs for your own unique situation.

IN LIVING COLOUR

As it sounds, living wills only affect you while you're alive, not at death. They specifically outline your medical wishes: how you'd want to be treated in case you become incapacitated or unable to make decisions. Hospital bills tend to be ridiculously expensive, so if you don't want to burden your family with them, you can choose to "pull the plug".

In a living will, you can also name what medical treatments you're willing or not willing to undergo, name a Healthcare Power of Attorney to make decisions for you, and add a DNR (do not resuscitate) if you wish.

SIMPLE WILL

This is the most common type of will. These estate docs direct how you would like your assets to be treated after you die and to whom they should be distributed. Unlike: Takeoff, 2pac, Nate Dogg, Prince, Bob Marley, and Jimi Hendrix. Typically, a simple will names an executor or trustee to manage your estate. This person handles admin duties like closing out accounts, paying outstanding debts, and then distributing the remaining assets.

GOT KIDS?

If you have any minor children, like Nate Dogg or Bob Marley prolifically had, you name a guardian for your children in your simple will. If no legal guardian is named, your minor children become wards of the state until a surviving parent or next of kin is located. Why would you let that happen? Do your family right and get a simple will.

TESTAMENTARY TRUST

A testamentary trust (or TT) is created by a will after death- like a caterpillar to a butterfly. Also known as a "will trust" or "trust under will", this is a trust that one's assets are transferred to and the named trustee manages and ultimately distributes the assets according to the will's instructions.

TT's are most useful when you have minor children (less than age 18) as your beneficiaries and will need help managing their inheritance. This trust allows you to add certain conditions on who, when, and how assets are distributed. Think: When the minor turns 18, they get a lump sum of blank $'s, when they graduate college, they get another lump sum of blank $'s, and when they buy their first car or house, they a remaining lump sum of blank $'s. There can be a named, triggering event that allows a distribution of money to the beneficiary.

Why? What do you think a traumatized 18-year-old would do with $1million?

OTHERS NOT RECOMMENDED

If you're more of the type of person who waits till the last minute, or who doesn't want to pay any proactive estate fees, or possibly even a gambler, these two will types may suit you, but not the court. Since these aren't witnessed nor made with any legal considerations, it's a high possibility they're worth what you paid — nada.

HOLOGRAPHIC WILLS

Not to be confused with the hologram 2Pac live concert technology that was unveiled a few years back. A Holographic Will is just a fancy way of saying a "handwritten". These can include whatever instructions one has for their assets, like a simple will, but there aren't any witnesses or signatures, these can be deemed invalid or thrown out in court by an unhappy person that had thought they'd be inheriting a paper stack or two. Also, in certain states, these types of wills aren't considered valid aka not worth the paper they're printed on.

ORAL WILLS

Can we please rename these to "spoken" wills instead of legalese-sounding nuncupative wills? Oral wills usually happen when you've completely neglected your estate planning and shout out your last wishes for your assets right before you die. Obviously, these spoken wills have strict requirements by the state to be considered valid at all. For instance, in North Carolina, their state laws allow for oral wills if death is imminent, so one doesn't have time to go through a formal will process.

Basically, oral wills are straight gambling with your wishes as they can be either thrown out as not valid by your state or easily contested. In other words, anyone can say you were crazy when you left them out of your spoken will.

– COMPLEX LEGAL –

TRUST YOU?

Say "trust fund" and I bet you think of "trust fund babies", i.e. entitled kids who don't need to work because someone put a bunch of money in an account for them to sponge off of. That's not the world I come from, and I bet you didn't either. A family trust is an alternative to a simple will, more expensive and detailed, but let's see if it's a fit for you first.

The funny thing about family trusts is that they are created when there's a lack of trust. Like you don't trust your heirs or future heirs to make good financial decisions, or you don't trust the government to tax and spend your hard-earned money, one last time when you die. Makes a lot of sense for people with a lot of means.

Unlike wills, family trusts are legal documents that effectively create a new "person" out of thin air, with a tax ID number, that owns your assets. This is exactly a version of what John D. Rockefeller set up for his family, and what most wealthy families utilize to legally escape "death taxes" and put restraints on distributions. If set up correctly, they can help keep your paper in your family and out of the government's pockets.

FUNCTION AT THE JUNCTION

All family trusts have certain roles that must be filled, so choose wisely. Typically, there are only three parties in a trust:

1. Grantor: the person who creates the trust and funds it with their assets.
2. Trustee: the person responsible for managing the assets on behalf of the beneficiaries.
3. …and Beneficiaries: people who will receive financial assets from the trust.

If you think of it in classic basketball terms, the grantor was Michael Jordan, and the trustee was Coach Phil Jackson, and the beneficiaries were 1990's Chicago Bulls fans… or you can make a great case for Nike, but that's a different story entirely.

TYPE A OR B

There are two basic types of trusts: revocable or irrevocable, and they both are used to transfer ownership of assets so that you stay out of probate court. That's the key with trusts, you don't own anything, and your estate stays out of probate court.

TRUSTS: REVOCABLE OR IRREVOCABLE?

REVOCABLE (MOST COMMON)

Revocable trusts can be changed, or revoked, when you see fit. The trust itself still owns the assets you transfer into it, but the names and instructions can be updated as life changes. Since you can alter these, the tax benefits are lower, but they still keep your heirs out of court and your wishes intact.

IRREVOCABLE

On the other hand, irrevocable trusts (or ITs) cannot be changed or altered. They're like putting footprints in fresh concrete- once dried, always there. ITs are set up with well-thought-out directions, never to be altered even if life changes, so choose wisely. Because they cannot be updated, they receive the largest tax benefits. Suffice to say, this is what John D. Rockefeller set up for his family, and what I guess former Roc-a-fella records icon and exec Jay-Z has set up for his family.

WHY ASK WHY?

Why do you need a family trust? Either you're really, really rich and want your family to stay that way, or you have another situation that requires one:

IT'S ALIVE!

A living trust is a type of family trust that holds your assets while you are still alive, in addition to providing instructions for what happens to your assets after you die. Many people do this to show they don't own anything but still control their assets. Be your own puppet master.

MARRIED WITH... OR WITHOUT KIDS

A marital trust is a special, irrevocable trust that benefits only the grantor's spouse- no one else. This trust avoids incurring federal taxes when it's transferred 100% from the grantor to the beneficiary. Typically, there are limits after the spouse dies, but the kids will have to fend for themselves or hire a great estate attorney.

GET RICH AND DIE GIVIN'

A charitable trust is created if a grantor wants to leave assets to a specific charity, either upfront or at the end. You'll get some tax deductions for your generosity and the ability to support a good cause you believe in.

SPECIAL NEEDS

If you have a child with special needs, they can collect government benefits, but only if they meet certain federal guidelines on available income and assets. The goal? Show they make little to no income and have a trust own their assets that only pay out for certain allowable costs, like medications, so those government benefits are not lost. You can't be there forever for your kids, but a special needs trust can.

– BASIC LEGAL –

POA ME

Last, but certainly not least, for your legal needs are the Power of Attorney (POAs). POAs can be used independently or with proper wills and trust. What's a POA?

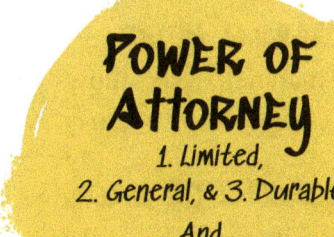

1. They give no power to an actual attorney,
2. They are recognized in every state, but the rules and requirements vary, and
3. Are powerless if you arrive D.O.A.

A power of attorney is a legal document that allows someone else to act on your behalf, called an agent. Think: When a big-time athlete scores a big-time contract, their super-agent has negotiated the new deal.

POAs give certain-named individuals certain-named powers, as if it were you making the decisions for yourself. The catch? They're generally only valid while you're alive, but either absent, cognitively impaired or incapacitated (like: old and confused or in a coma). You die? They become worthless and either your will, trust, or probate takes over.

There are three basic types of POA's: limited, general, and durable.

LIMITED EDITION

A Limited POA is most common and can only be used for a specific purpose only. There are a few types:

A. GET SPRUNG

A "Springing POA" only can be utilized by an agent(s) when a specific condition is met. For example, an armed forces member should create a springing power of attorney to be prepared in case of being deployed so that family members back home can be granted power to make financial or legal decisions on their behalf.

B. FINANCIAL MOVES

A "Financial POA" allows your agent to make decisions only about your money and property. Nothing else, nothing more.

C. MEDICINAL OR CHRONIC

A "Healthcare POA" allows your agent to make your healthcare decisions for you when you cannot. You formally would write down your wishes to be crudely kept "plugged in" or "unplugged". Don't have one? Then someone else, like an ex-spouse, or an action group with a vested interest may do it for you.

GENERAL TSO'S

A General POA validates your agent(s) all of your powers and rights, and can be used for managing finances, collecting debts, and applying for credit cards; but ends if you become incapacitated (like in a coma).

DURABLE GOODS

A Durable POA does everything a General POA does but remains in power even if the individual becomes incapacitated. This is considered to be the most powerful type of POA.

...AND LASTLY, GIVE IT TO ME DIRECT

An Advance Medical Directive is a legal document that gives instructions for your medical care only if you cannot communicate your own wishes. The two most common advance directives for health care are the living will, and the durable power of attorney for health care.

JUST START WITH THE BASICS

Confused yet? Great, that's how the attorneys want you. Legalese is a language made only for attorneys and paying clients, so research what you need and have a reputable lawyer make only what you need. Only agree to a reasonable, fixed price— not a meter running for every phone call, text, or email. Get organized, be specific, and get something in place.

If you need a great place to start that covers the basics, get yourself a:

• Simple Will,
• Financial and Healthcare POA's and an
• Advanced Medical Directive.

You can always add, edit, or remove these documents as life changes. Just get something in place first. Your loved ones won't be sorry.

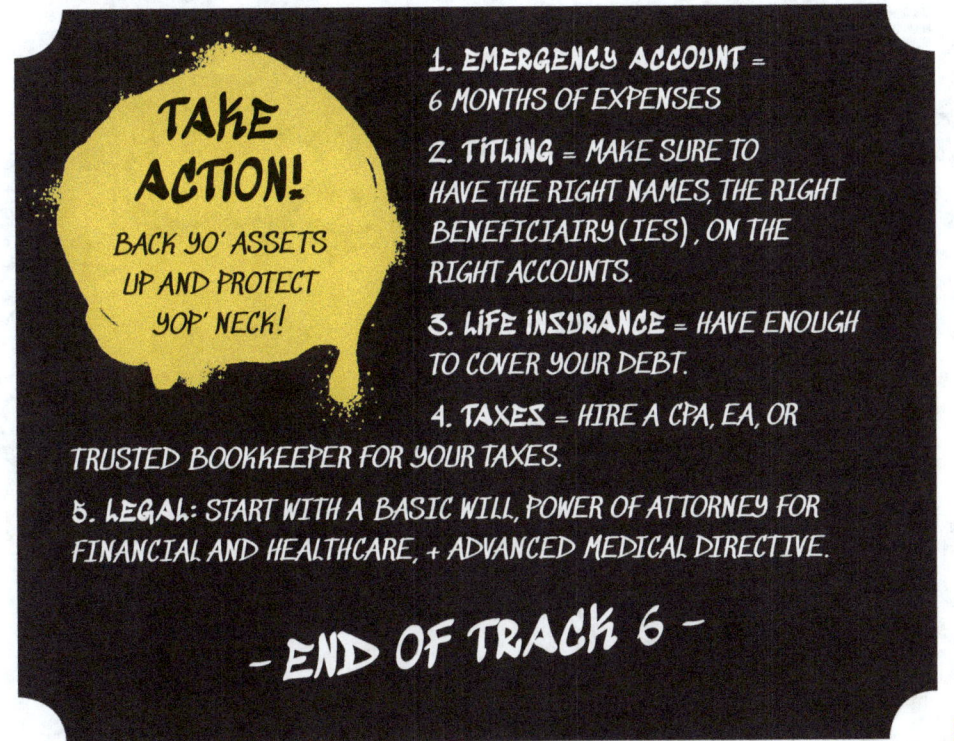

SIMPLE WILL

FINANCIAL & HEALTHCARE POA'S

MEDICAL DIRECTIVE

TITLING AND BENEFICIARIES

TAKE ACTION!

BACK YO' ASSETS UP AND PROTECT YOP' NECK!

1. **EMERGENCY ACCOUNT** = 6 MONTHS OF EXPENSES

2. **TITLING** = MAKE SURE TO HAVE THE RIGHT NAMES, THE RIGHT BENEFICIAIRY (IES), ON THE RIGHT ACCOUNTS.

3. **LIFE INSURANCE** = HAVE ENOUGH TO COVER YOUR DEBT.

4. **TAXES** = HIRE A CPA, EA, OR TRUSTED BOOKKEEPER FOR YOUR TAXES.

5. **LEGAL:** START WITH A BASIC WILL, POWER OF ATTORNEY FOR FINANCIAL AND HEALTHCARE, + ADVANCED MEDICAL DIRECTIVE.

- END OF TRACK 6 -

TRACK 7. STRAIGHT OUTTA COMPOUND

TRACK 7: STRAIGHT OUTTA COMPOUND

> "Compound interest is the eight wonder of the world. He who understands it, makes it, he who doesn't pays it."

-Albert Einstein

Want to know how to legally double your money, time, and legacy? Compound interest. One more time for the people in the back: compound interest. You need to make your paperwork for you, and ensure your interests get compounded.

Here's some time-tested knowledge that's so easy to say, but so hard to put into practice: "If you want to get anywhere, you have to start somewhere." There isn't a good time to do anything, you just have to get started. This is what happens when compound interest is paid out after your first deposit at a bank or when an investment increases in value over time.

Only the future knows what your compounded interests will become. Just remember this: We all have the same amount of time in the day to get where we want to go. Your choices will determine your outcome.

You get to decide to stop digging that hole you were in.
You have the power to make better money decisions.
You can decide to out hustle your competition.
You should be able to spend and save wisely.

Your investments can pay you back with time and comfort. Your smart planning will help insure your finances, legal, and taxes. You get to compound your life and legacy, just as I did in writing this book. I've tried to take everything I've learned in the personal finance game, distill it down, and mix it up with hip-hop to make a drink you can enjoy and share with friends. That's how knowledge spreads.

What are you going to do with your future?

Dre came "Straight Outta Compton" before becoming the G.O.A.T hip-hop producer behind N.W.A, Snoop, 2pac, Eminem, and Kendrick Lamar; making a mint off Beats by Dre, and performing one of the most epic Super Bowl halftime shows in 2022. Jay-Z had "99 Problems" until he became widely regarded as the "greatest rapper of all time", became the richest rap mogul in history, and married Beyoncé to become a modern-day King and Queen of hip-hop and RnB.

What if you "Lose Yourself" in the music, the moment, and own it? Eminem did; he transcended fear, race, and the Detroit projects to become a global phenom and the number one, top-selling hip-hop artist of all time.

Drake "Started from the Bottom" in Toronto, and now he's on top; flying Air Drake around for free giving "God's Plan" to his fans with free tickets and cash to pay off student loans, mortgages, and health bills.

A lot of rappers discussed in this book got their futures cut short due to bad choices or found themselves in some serious financial sh*t. What would 2pac, Biggie, Nipsey Hustle, or Takeoff have done with more time?

If they could've gone back in time and made better financial choices, what would Lil' Kim, DMX, Nelly, Nas, MC Hammer, 50 Cent, Ja Rule, Method Man, Lauryn Hill, and Fat Joe have done to not end up in bankruptcy court? We all only have so much time in this game called life and many decisions to make—for better or worse. Educate yourself and play the long game. Always keep compounding.

Now that you're learning to master your zeros and commas, you can be ready for how to compound your resources. How you spend your time and wealth and craft your legacy is important. Do not forget that money is a tool and it's your tool to do these things. Money doesn't buy happiness but can make life easier. Finding your purpose here on planet Earth is what will create your happiness. If you do nothing, I guarantee you a predictably, boring existence of "should've, could've, and would've."

Get out there and make something of yourself. Become someone others can look up to and ask questions, inspiring them to reinvent the circle for themselves. If you can make some stacks along the way, keep your mind on your money, but use it to pursue happiness- whatever that means to you.

TIME

Like Ice Cube said, "Chiggity-Check Yourself Before You Wreck Yourself," and be able to say, "It Was A Good Day".

Time is the most valuable asset there is, followed by information and money. How you spend your time is different when you're young versus when you get older. The trappings of youth and living fast can lead to mistakes, that if you don't learn from, can cost you dearly—or your life like 2pac, Biggie, Nipsey Hustle, and Takeoff. Experience life, make mistakes you can learn from, and add it to your life resume. Spend your time learning both in and out of the classroom. Stay curious, seeking answers to the problems you see.

When I was younger, like most, I had a lot of time and no money. That limited my ability to experience the fullness of life, so I had to put in the work first and learn before I earned. I struggled, hustled, and made plenty of mistakes, but eventually found my purpose and career in finance. Now I have mo' money and less time. It's only come full circle now, 30 years later, that my love of drumming, the beats, and the music has been combined with my finance career to create this book. All good things take time.

THE CHOICES YOU MAKE ON HOW TO SPEND YOUR TIME COMPOUND INTO WHAT YOUR LIFE WILL BECOME.

I couldn't write this book, spend time with my family, go on vacations, or go to concerts without having the means to do it. Taking the same advice I give my clients daily has allowed me to save up first and spend second. Money gives you options on how to spend your time—maybe that's taking time off to relax, volunteer, create, focus on your health, or make memories. The beauty of options is that you have them. Without it, you barely get by, wish you'd hit the lottery, or blame others for your misfortunes.

A couple of years ago, my wife and I were celebrating our 10th anniversary back in Italy. She got caught up looking back 10 years and being a good financial planner, I was caught up looking forward 10 years. Our wedding day was magical and worth every ounce of time we spent on it, so I got my wife's nostalgia, but I couldn't help thinking about what life would be like 10 years down the line. Our daughters, ages seven and eight then, would be on their way into the world seeking their life's purpose. Knowing the stat that you spend 80% of your time with your parents from the crib to age 18, and then only 20% for the rest of your life—it scared the hell out of me. What if I don't have 10 years? Will my parents be here? The pressure was building. How could I squeeze out more time for my family and friends in the next 10 years before life happens?

Answer: I moved my office closer to home.

LOCATION, LOCATION, LOCATION

Remote work post-pandemic has certainly helped a lot of people stay flexible and at home. Instead of my usual hour drive time per day, I opened an office right down the street. A whopping 2-minute commute! How much time did I get reclaim back? Five hours a week, or 260 hours a year, for a total of 32+ freed up days per year. I wisely invested some of my future money per month into office rent that guarantees me an entire month-plus back for whatever I choose to do with my time. What a beautiful trade of money vs. time. That's the difference between working hard and working smart. I get more time to focus on what I'm good at, spend more time with my wife and daughters, and get a good outdoor walk-in when the mood strikes. It's a win-win-win.

If you hustle younger in life, save, and then can afford time-off, you'll get a chance to re-configure your life to how you see fit. What works for me isn't necessarily what will work for you, but having the option through savings can afford you more time.

LEARN TO SAY "NO"

Jesse Itzler, the king of entrepreneurial hustle from Chapter 3 would tell you to say "YES" to every opportunity that comes your way when you're getting started. Just showing up and being in the right place at the right time is half the battle. How do you think he got all his NYC connections from Alphabet City like Jam Master Jay, 50 Cent, and Jay-Z? Sitting around? Hell no. He hustled and got in front of the right people even if it meant spending a mint on Yankees tickets. What about Marquis Jet? That never would've happened if he took "NO" for an answer. There would've been no connection made with Matt Damon that ended up helping him with Zico Coconut Water, or most importantly his wife Sara Blakely. If you don't ask, it's always a "no", but if you take "no" for an answer, you didn't try hard enough.

Guess what Jesse Itzler does now? He says "no" a lot.

Not to opportunity, but to anything that costs him time away from his individual mission of purpose. He puts family first, then extreme athletic adventures, bucket list ideas, and speaking engagements, all on one big-*ss, 12-month calendar, allowing him to visualize his year ahead. If you're not on that calendar, better luck next year.

Do you think most successful people do the exact same thing? Yes, it's called time-blocking. The act of making a workable, daily schedule that's balanced and fulfilling to you. After he went from hip-hop to Hollywood, Mark Wahlberg of "Good Vibrations" fame (by Marky-Mark and the Funky Bunch), started a now legendary, daily schedule that goes from 2:30am to 7:30pm. Do a quick search to get some pointers.

I follow Jesse Itzler on Instagram and subscribe to his newsletter, where I take note of his extreme time-blocking techniques. For me, three months out is my ideal number; not too short and not too far out to plan ahead. Let's face it, no one is getting any younger.

Want to know the secret of saying "no"? If you don't respect my time enough to plan ahead and are not on my calendar, then it's a respectable "no". If you really want to get on there, then I know you'll try again later. If not, we didn't waste each other's time. Learn to say "no". I don't know how much time it will save you exactly, but a lot. If you become successful, you'll need all the time you can find.

SURROUND YOURSELF WITH GREAT PEOPLE

One of the biggest ways to maximize your time is by surrounding yourself with the right people. You don't get to choose your family, but if you water your own lawn, the grass will get greener. I've been lucky enough to share countless amounts of time and make lasting memories with my wife and daughters. For my immediate family, it's grown tougher after I left home at age 18, but we focus on quality time these days, not quantity of time. You do you.

You do get to choose your friends and your employees if you're an entrepreneur. Friends are easy when life is, say, before children. When life gets hard, like during COVID shutdowns, you'll find out who your real friends are. If you're lucky enough, you'll have one true best friend you can be there for and vice versa. Shoutout to my best friend- you're the reason this book took years. Much love brother!

Employees are the people you choose to surround yourself with five days a week. They get more time than your family does, albeit work time, but more time than anyone else. Is there any reason to have a bad employee then? Hell no. We're all human and have bad days, but not bad weeks. If you have the wrong attitude consistently, then a boss who values their time will replace you with someone who brings the right attitude to work. For you aspiring hustlers: show up and show out. Do you really think Dr. Dre, Rick Rubin, or any of the greatest producers take on artists who don't bring their A-game? If you value yourself and your work ethic, chances are high that your boss will too.

My assistant may have been fresh out of college with much to learn when I hired her, but her daily, positive attitude is a win-win for my business and my clients. Even if my clients or I are frustrated in the moment, the right attitude soothes the situation until those feelings subside or a problem is course corrected. She saves me so much time by showing up and showing out that I get to focus on what I'm best at and even better yet, spend that extra time with my loved ones.

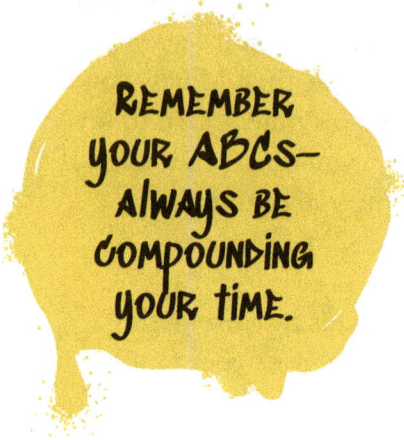

REMEMBER your ABCs— always be compounding your time.

Remember your ABCs—always be compounding your time.

TAKE TIME FOR SELF-CARE

This last one is new for me. After years of the hustle and successful growth, working more and more for that aspirational American Dream, you will get burnt out. Some people go decades before the wheels come off, but at what cost?

My wife is the opposite of me: a nurturing, artist-type, free of time and money constraints. She's as Zen and balanced as they come. Even when she's averagely upset, she won't yell at me. She taught me about nutrition and cooks our meals by hand strictly following the "you are what you eat" mantra. She also practices the art of not being over-scheduled and yoga to practice turning off your mind and being present in the now. I try my best to achieve balance, but it's usually fleeting. Maybe my balance is found in the act of trying, but you should at least try.

There is significant power in someone who is mentally and physically healthy; someone who takes time to practice "self-care", even if Mac Miller didn't get the help he needed to understand a healthy way to stay balanced. A lot of the first responder community I get to work with, see things us "normal" people don't have to and take the edge off with alcohol. There are so many better natural ways to stay mentally and physically healthy that lead to balance rather than unhealthy habits that only waste away your time.

Find your balance and take pride in each day you get to have. Practice the gratitude attitude. Always be thinking of how you can free yourself from those monotonous duties to free up your time. It's more precious than anything. Once you learn that, your investment in time will be compounded over and over again.

WEALTH

Money is a tool, but true wealth comes from accumulated assets and wisdom. If you've read this book and then put it into practice- you've made your first moves. By the amount of mentions in this book, throw on Jay-Z's 4:44 album and we'll call it even. There's street wisdom on tap in so many of his rhymes, hence why he has the highest net worth.

Your wealth or "net worth" measures the value of everything you "own" minus what you "owe". It can be calculated for any individual, company, or country. For example:

Notice how wealth doesn't have anything to do with one's cash flow (that's income - expenses)? You can have higher or lower income and debts and still have a higher net worth. This is exactly how compound interest works. What you have in accumulated assets keeps growing larger, your debts stay fixed, and your income either goes up or down.

Remember those online bank High-Yield Savings Accounts? They're an easy

JAY-Z
WEALTHIEST RAPPER

$2.5 BILLION

APPLE
MOST VALUABLE COMPANY

$3.4 TRILLION

USA
WEALTHIEST COUNTRY

$164 TRILLION

All data current November 2024

example of how compound interest works in tangible assets: Assets that you can see, touch, and feel. Bank accounts, if left alone, do not go substantially up or down in value like stocks, real estate, or collectibles-they only gain compound interest.

LET'S MAKE SOME BANK

Let's say you deposit $1,000 in an online bank HYSA.

How much cash is stacked on Year 1? Answer = $1,040.00 or +$40.00.
How much cash is stacked on Year 2? Answer = $1,081.60 or +$41.60.
How much cash is stacked on Year 3? Answer = $1,124.86 or +$43.26.

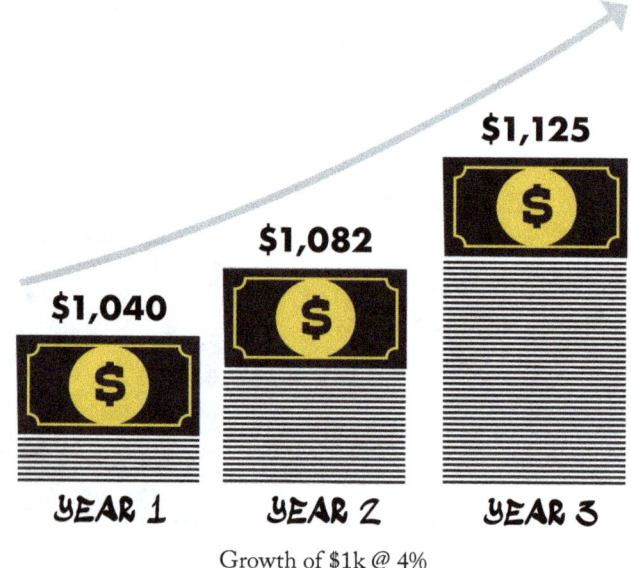

Growth of $1k @ 4%

Do you see how the parentheses numbers start at $40, then $41.60, and then $43.26? Compound interest grows off the last number, not the first. It gives you a built-in raise every year. This is how if you add a few more commas and zeros, I bet I'll keep your attention longer.

Let's deposit $1 million in a HYSA with the same 4% rate.

Year 1: $1,040,000 or +$40,000
Year 2: $1,081,600 or +$41,600
Year 3: $1,124,860 or +$43,260

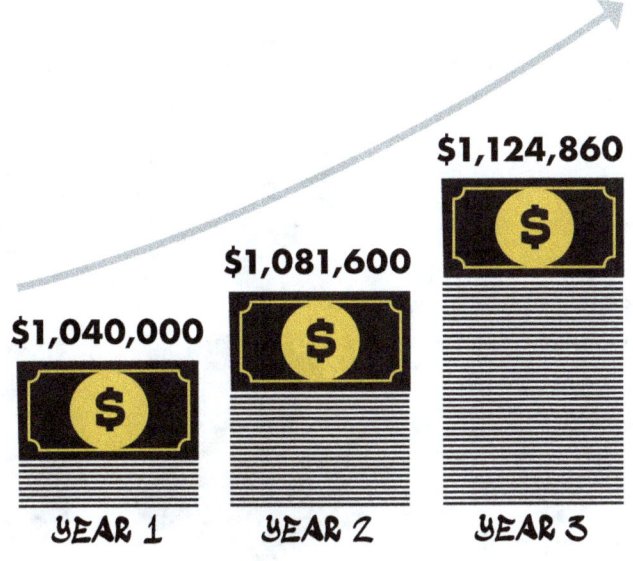

Growth of $1M @ 4%

That's a good chunk of a blue-collar job's annual pay just from compound interest in a bank account. Y'all wonder how the rich get richer? They understand how compound interest works and let their money work for them. That's the not-so-secret sauce. Accumulate real wealth and let it work for you by compounding every year.

WHIP YOU INTO SHAPE

Here's a real-life situation: You want to buy a normal whip that gets you from Point A to Point B each day. Two examples of how to buy it:

Person A gets a loan to buy a $50,000 car that costs $1,000 per month.

Person B buys an Airbnb property that pays $1,000 per month in cash flow that pays the monthly car payment.

Can you spot the difference in technique?

Person A takes an additional debt payment per month for a depreciating asset that goes down in value. At the end of five years, there is no value or $0 left to compound.

Person B invests in an appreciating Airbnb property that goes up in value, with a fixed loan, and that rent received pays for their monthly whip payment. Also, if they use said whip for their rental business, it can be deducted from their taxes. At the end of five years, they drove their car for free and their home equity went up. They were compounding $'s from day one and will continue to add to it.

Are your interests in wealth getting compounded yet? I hope so, because this is how wealth works for you and your family. Understand it and make it work for you, or stay the dumb money that pay it to the banks. Think like a bank or from Jay-Z's "Moment of Clarity".

> **"**When your cents got that much in common,
> And you been hustling since your inception,
> F*ck perception! Go with what makes sense,
> Since I know what I'm up against,
> We as rappers must decide what's most important**"**

Compound interest.

INTANGIBLE WEALTH

Wealth comes from the accumulation of not only real assets, but knowledge and other intangible assets. What's an example of an intangible asset?

• How about every hip-hop line Nas ever wrote?
• How about Travis Scott's ability to perform in front of millions?
• How about building and crafting a personal brand from nothing like Kanye's Yeezy's?

All of these intangible assets are called "intellectual property".

WHAT IS INTELLECTUAL PROPERTY?

According to the World Intellectual Property Organization, Intellectual property (or IP) refers to creations of the mind, such as inventions; literary and artistic works; designs; and symbols, names and images used in commerce.

As much as a hip-hop song is the artist's intellectual property, so are Elon Musk's cars and rockets, or a miracle weight loss drug for a pharmaceutical company. They're all worth mountains of paper stacks and protected by trademarks and patents. Intellectual capital can be worth a lot and adds significant wealth to a person or company's net worth.

Isn't it ironic then that rappers creating intellectual property are usually made by bragging about all of their tangible property or real "stuff" like ice, whips, grills, chains, and cribs? But not always, here's a classic musicology tale about a former superstar who bought a supergroup's catalog of music.

MJ BUYS THE BEATLES

Back in 1982, during the early days of hip-hop, the best-selling pop album of all time, Thriller, was released by Michael Jackson. Not only did it crown him the "King of Pop", but it made him a lot of money in the process. Looking to invest that money, he had all kinds of options. One that he hadn't considered before was the idea of music publishing—owning another musician's intellectual property rights to their music. Why?

For licensing purposes. Every time a commercial uses a song or it gets streamed, the owner of the publishing rights gets paid. That's big money over a long time if you can acquire the right music. No different than why Taylor Swift re-recorded her records- she owns outright her "Taylor's Versions". It's also why artists like Bob Dylan, Justin Bieber, Paul Simon, David Bowie, Sting, and Stevie Nicks have gotten paid hundreds of millions of dollars for their catalogs. Purely hip-hop related, the producer Metro Boomin', known for Migos, Drake, and Future records, sold a portion of his catalog to Shamrock Capital for $70 million in early 2023.

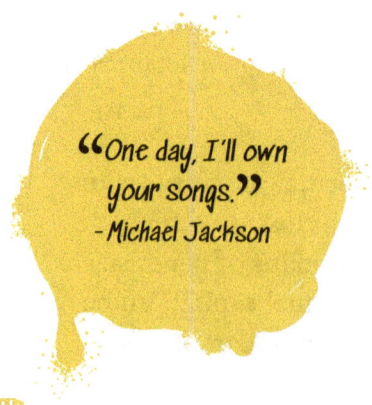

"One day, I'll own your songs."
- Michael Jackson

No one is paying that amount of money if there isn't a lot more paper to be made. Investors who understand compound interest understand the power of long-term investment growth.

Back to MJ. The legend goes that when Michael was doing a duet with Paul McCartney on his record "Say, Say, Say", Paul bragged about buying music publishing rights with his Beatles money.

MJ's alleged response, "One day, I'll own your songs". Two years and $47 million dollars later- he did just that. MJ bought The Beatles' entire catalog, outbidding Sir Paul himself. While it cost him a friendship (Paul allegedly never spoke to him again), MJ's purchase turned into the greatest investment he ever made: A whopping $1+ billion. Now you can understand why music publishing and intangible assets are BIG business.

MY BEST INVESTMENTS WEREN'T INVESTMENTS.

Being in the investment business and understanding compound interest in my sleep, I'll make a bold statement. My best investments weren't investments, and your best investments probably won't be "investments" either.

I can preach all day about "investments", saving, and planning ahead. I've become a balance sheet millionaire by living out my own advice that I share with my clients. I have an emergency savings which I dub the "Oh Sh*t" account, several different retirement accounts, a residence, a getaway property, saving for my kid's college, and tax-free ROTH IRA accounts. Doing the boring stuff over and over really works on paper—there really isn't much of an investment risk if you have a long time period in front of you. That's the beauty of being young, you theoretically have a lot of time.

No, my biggest investment returns were from taking personal chances- the intangible asset kind that adds to one's personal wealth: skills, experiences, connections, and education.

WHAT IF'S

What if I didn't hear my first hip-hop record in junior high while shooting hoops? I wouldn't have gotten addicted to the beats and melodies which led directly to becoming a drummer. Growing up in Northeast Ohio white farmlands, I also wouldn't have been culturally exposed to Arrested Development, Kriss Kross, Cross Colours clothing, Dwayne Wayne's flip glasses, or Fresh Prince of Bel-Air. That was a special time in my life where I found out I liked different music and cultures not being shown to me.

What if I didn't learn how to play drums in high school? If I hadn't learned how to play and play with confidence, I wouldn't have become at ease with stage fright, and eventually public speaking. I wouldn't have met my college friends, who were virtually all from being in bands and playing out. I most certainly wouldn't have been able to spend time in Williamsburg-Brooklyn as it was turning over in the mid-2000s. The cultural exposure from the Big Apple helped me learn the hustle, think bigger, and learn that the cream rises to the top.

What if I didn't go to Ohio State University? I wouldn't have had the social opportunities that led to meeting my friends, musical opportunities, and experiencing the late 1990s hip-hop blow-up. I also would've missed my first internship at Merrill Lynch, where I got exposed to my second love of finance and learned to thrive under pressure.

What if I didn't have a "Year of Saying Yes" in 2010 after nearly losing it all in the Great Financial Crisis? Would I still have met my German wife, who introduced me to a new culture across the Atlantic, led to regular international travel, and allowed us to raise our daughters as bilingual? Not to mention being my rock—the voice of sanity and calmness when you go from being married to having children. Or being honest and telling me when one of my crazy idea's sucks. Take it from me: Your partner in life is the biggest and most impactful decision you'll make. It will either compound your life for the better or worse, so take your time and choose wisely.

What if I didn't go back to school for my CERTIFIED FINANCIAL PLANNER® in late 2019? I could've easily said that at age 40 I was "too old" or "it won't make a difference" or "I don't have the time to do an accelerated nine-month course". Turns out everyone had all the time in the world when the pandemic shut down normal life. I didn't notice until I passed my exam the first time in November of 2020. Coincidence? I think not.

Lastly, what if I didn't take the risk of writing this book? What began as a simple bucket-list goal turned into an opportunity to share who I am—in both music and a finance, a creative and a businessman—and the wisdom I've gained from over 20 years in the finance industry.

The compound interest you will earn from taking personal chances throughout your life will author the book you write and how you want to be remembered. Revisiting Jay-Z's "Moment of Clarity" line once more, we can end this book on "legacy":

> *"And I can't help the poor if I'm one of them.*
> *So, I got rich and gave back,*
> *to me that's the win-win."*

LEGACY

Once you've reached some success in life, or become a parent, or do something of worth with your time, you may start thinking of your death and the legacy you'll leave behind. How this game of life will remember you. For me, it was early mid-life: sometime after my first niece was born, seeing your parents' age, and losing your grandparents. Life gets real in the middle, so it's natural to find an escape or think about when you become your parents and then your grandparents. My escape was thinking about how to pay it forward in a way that was right for me.

You can either give money, time, education, or love- all can pay out compound interest to the future generations. In the end, we are merely renting everything we have until time takes it from us. As Ernest Hemingway said, "Every man has two deaths, when he is buried in the ground and the last time someone says his name." Hemingway would've been a bad*ss rapper. If you're an aspiring lyricist, check out his life and books. You'll be entertained and educated.

I don't know about the truth of two deaths, but we can certainly do something at any time we're alive that pays out compound interest to others instead of to ourselves. As Jay-Z rhymes it, this tends to be after we accumulate wealth that we look to give it back. Plus, the CFP® in me knows that in the U.S.A., you get some nice tax breaks for charitable giving. Don't hate the playa, hate the game.

CASH MONEY CARNEGIE

One of history's richest men, not named Rockefeller, was Andrew Carnegie. You might've heard of Carnegie Hall in Manhattan? The Scottish-born immigrant came to America at the age 12 with his parents in 1842. He became an incredibly successful businessman, and an industrialist who introduced steel to the world through his company, US Steel.

How?

In 1874, after building the Eads Bridge in St. Louis completely out of his steel, he needed to prove the new material was safe. At that time, the bridge was the longest rail and road bridge in the world and connected the east to the west. Knowing the legend that elephants won't cross an unstable bridge, Carnegie rented one from a traveling circus and led a parade across. The people were astonished, and orders came flooding in. Elon Musk must've studied showmanship from Carnegie.

Carnegie went on to make US Steel the largest steel company in the world and sold it to JP Morgan (you know his banks) in 1901. How much? For the whopping current-day lump sum equivalent of $11.2 trillion dollars. He instantly became the richest American in history—passing John D. Rockefeller. What'd he do for an encore?

The last 20 years of his life he spent putting his last name on education and the arts; giving away 90% of his wealth to establishing universities, schools, upwards of 3,000 free public libraries across the English-speaking world. He also donated nearly 7,000 church organs to churches and civic organizations. He single-handedly inspired Warren Buffett and Bill Gates' modern-day Giving Pledge; where the world's wealthiest people publicly commit to give the majority of their wealth to philanthropy, either during their lifetimes or in their wills.

Guess what?

The Eads bridge is still in use today like many of his schools and libraries. That's a legacy investment that has been paying compound interest for generations.

TEACH THEM TO FISH

According to Oxford Languages, the definition of philanthropy is, "the desire to promote the welfare of others, expressed especially by the generous donation of money to good causes. Using one's amassed wealth can make life better for countless people, creating opportunities that didn't exist before, and paying it forward with personal legacy." Give a man a fish and he eats for a day. Teach a man to fish and he'll eat the rest of his life.

In the same vein as Carnegie, here's a short list of rappers who are giving back to their communities to make them better: Follow their passions and follow their lead of giving back. If you don't get to the same level of wealth, remember, you still can give your time. Be a mentor or pass on the gratitude attitude in your community.

JAY-Z

You'd expect the wealthiest rapper to be the most charitable. Back in 2003, and long before becoming a billionaire, Jay-Z established The Shawn Carter Foundation to help people get into post-secondary institutions despite socio-economic hardships that they may face. On its 20th anniversary, The Shawn Carter Foundation black tie gala raised $20 million.

In 2006, he headlined a concert in which he raised over $250,000 for Water for People, a charity that helps developing countries provide clean, drinking water. In 2012, he headlined a hip-hop series at that same Carnegie Hall, where he raised millions of dollars for the United Way of New York City and his foundation.

He also flat-out wrote a $1 million check to the American Red Cross after the destruction of Hurricane Katrina for relief efforts. To push his cause of reading and education, he also sponsored the Book of HOV tribute exhibition at the Brooklyn Public Library. The exhibition highlighted his come-up from the Marcy Projects to worldwide fame and business acumen, with the message: always bet on yourself.

That's compound interest in action using time, money, and personal connections to support your causes.

DR. DRE

When you get Apple money, you should plant an orchard- and that's just what Dre did. In 2013, along with co-creator of Beats, Jimmy Iovine, they combined forces and donated $70 million to the University of Southern California. Why? To create a brand-new, four-year program for undergraduates who are interested in computer science and engineering, the arts, marketing, audio and visual design, and business entrepreneurship. Sounds similar to what they did with Beats, right?

The purpose of this program is to shape the minds of young students who challenge the conventional ways of industry and art. OK, definitely like what they did with Beats. No donation would be complete without adding your name to it, so what's the new academy called? The USC Jimmy Iovine and Andre Young Academy for Arts, Technology and the Business of Innovation. I hope they left some money for the sign.

WILL.I.AM

Will.i.am used his "Beats by Dre" investment earnings to fund his i.am.angel foundation. The mission is to "administer charitable activities and programs targeted towards providing college scholarships (i.am scholarship), college preparation (i.am College Track), and opportunities in STEAM education (Science, Technology, Engineering, Arts and Mathematics)."

QUEEN LATIFAH

The hip-hop female pioneer, actress, and philanthropist, Queen Latifah, has won a Grammy Award and a Golden Globe. She was also the first hip-hop artist to receive a star on the Hollywood Walk of Fame. In 1992, following the death of her brother in a motorcycle accident, the New Jersey native and her schoolteacher mother created the Lancelot H. Owens Scholarship Foundation. Choosing to make a dark moment shine bright, the foundation awards college scholarships to economically challenged students in low-income, underprivileged neighborhoods in the New York tri-state area. The purpose of the foundation is to provide opportunities in education and leadership development to youth with promising futures, but who have limited financial resources for secondary education. In order to receive the foundation's scholarship, all recipients are asked to give back to their communities through active volunteering and pay-it-forward mentoring.

Giving outside of her tri-state roots, Queen Latifah is also involved in Alicia Keys' charity, Keep a Child Alive, which provides medicine to people in Africa and India to help eradicate HIV-AIDS. It helps pay medical costs incurred by doctors in Haiti in order to provide better healthcare for their patients. Royalty setting the right example.

LUDACRIS

The Atlanta-based rapper, Ludacris, gained fame with 2000s "Southern Hospitality" and has given back ever since through The Ludacris Foundation. Its mission? To inspire under-served youth and inner-city communities to live their dreams and provide programs which create new experiences that help them envision their full potential. The LudaCares programs includes:

Day of Service that serves Feeding America and the Make-A-Wish Foundation, as well as visiting hospitals like Children's Hospital Atlanta or Walter Reed in Washington DC.

LudaDay is a stay-in-school program that features weekend activities, like celebrity basketball games and family park events.

LudaCares® Thanksgiving gives back to families in need by providing them with turkeys, nutritious vegetables, and the trimmings.

Ludacrismas® shares the Christmas cheer to underprivileged youth by providing gifts and holiday experiences for children and their families.

MISSY ELLIOT

Missy Elliott "Works It" for all kinds of worthwhile charities. She was the first hip-hop artist to perform at the all-female Lilith Fair tour. The tour raised millions of dollars for AIDS and breast cancer research, and she has since been active in many other charities raising even more money for AIDS research. Along with supermodel Iman, they created and sold a lipstick called "Misdemeanor Lipstick" where the money raised from sales went to Break the Cycle, a nonprofit with the goal of ending domestic violence in young individuals.

LIL' WAYNE

In 2007, despite his large tax problems at the time, Lil' Wayne started the 1 Family Foundation with a mission to empower underserved youth from low-income areas to develop their talents and skill sets. His foundation also educates these youth in ways to become economically productive and self-sufficient by encouraging them to dream beyond their current circumstances.

Weezy also stepped up when Hurricane Katrina devastated New Orleans in 2005, donating $200,000 to reconstruct a park that he played at in his childhood. Every Thanksgiving, he volunteers in the Cash Money annual turkey giveaway, providing local families in need with a holiday meal and fixings as well as providing free medical screenings.

RICK ROSS

After Rick Ross was "Hustlin", he purchased Evander Holyfield's Georgia estate: A 235-acre, 109-room mansion with an Olympic-sized swimming pool, horse stable, and baseball field. Sound familiar to 50 buying Mike Tyson's mansion? Hopefully, his cashflow game is on point because Ross' charitable plans include opening up this lavish estate to inner-city youth, providing them with a sort of countryside summer camp. The purpose is to get these youth out of their current environment and introduce positive education and influences into their lives.

Ross also brings the Christmas spirit to his hometown of Miami, hosting an annual Christmas Toy and Food Giveaway.

DRAKE

Before his recent "It's All a Blur" concert cash giveaways to fans, Drake first made headlines with his charitable work when his Scorpion album came out in 2018. How? He wrote checks for schools, scholarships, and went on an epic supermarket spending spree in Miami.

For Miami Senior High School, where he shot the "God's Plan" video, Drake first wrote a $25,000 check of gratitude and promised all-new school uniforms. A couple of days later, he randomly showed up at a local supermarket, where he reportedly spent $50,000 on groceries for the 50 customers inside the location, allowing them to get whatever they needed. Topping off his charitable giving, he surprised biology major Destiny James with a $50,000 scholarship and then performed at the Moss Terrace in the Donna E. Shalala Student Center. That's paying it forward on many levels and living "God's Plan".

Being a regular to charitable gifting, he's been known to give for hurricane relief, school supplies, and other charitable causes; like in 2022, when he donated $1 million in Bitcoin to LeBron James' I Promise school in Ohio.

Use the real-life lessons in this book to become a financial gangster and live financially authentic; don't "spend to pretend". Get off "Debt Row" to start your own financial journey like I did. I want my financial gang to graduate the "School of Hard Knocks" and get yourself wealthy through saving and investing to create opportunity for you and your family. Don't get tripped up on "Mo' Money, Mo Problems", stack your cash flow, and then remember to "Back Yo' Assets Up."

If you combine these rhymes, you too can create generational wealth and charitable gifting like John D. Rockefeller, Andrew Carnegie, or Warren Buffet. Get yourself in the position to go "Straight Outta

Compound" and pay it forward to your family, friends, and community.

Someday, I'd love to write a book about your story and how you were able to put your last name on your own foundation to give back.

I'm dropping the mic here so you can pick it up.

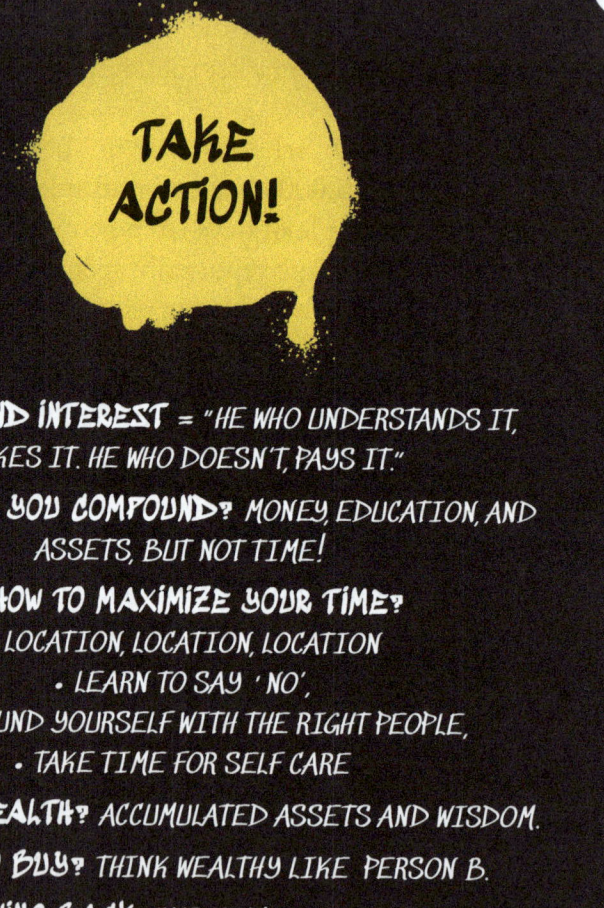

TAKE ACTION!

1. **COMPOUND INTEREST** = *"HE WHO UNDERSTANDS IT, MAKES IT. HE WHO DOESN'T, PAYS IT."*

2. **WHAT CAN YOU COMPOUND?** *MONEY, EDUCATION, AND ASSETS, BUT NOT TIME!*

3. **HOW TO MAXIMIZE YOUR TIME?**
   - *LOCATION, LOCATION, LOCATION*
   - *LEARN TO SAY 'NO',*
   - *SURROUND YOURSELF WITH THE RIGHT PEOPLE,*
   - *TAKE TIME FOR SELF CARE*

4. **WHAT IS WEALTH?** *ACCUMULATED ASSETS AND WISDOM.*

5. **HOW TO BUY?** *THINK WEALTHY LIKE PERSON B.*

6. **GIVING BACK.** *IT'S NOT PAYING BACK, IT'S PAYING IT FORWARD.*

– END OF TRACK 7 –

SHOUT-OUTS

To Johanna: you're my biggest supporter, my north star, and the partner I needed in life to grow-up. You keep it real every day. I need those encouragements to keep balanced, but above all- remember it's "work to live", not "live to work". Somehow though, I convince you to let me run down the occasional rabbit hole like "writing a book." Thank you my love.

To Lena and Elise: I hope Daddy's shown you girls how to properly chase down your dreams and turn them into reality. We love you both and the world is yours! Just remember, it's progress, not perfection. Because there's a parental advisory sticker, you'll have to wait until your teenagers to read this book.

To Mom and Dad: thank you all those years ago for gifting me that rabbit figurine holding the big carrot with the simple inscription reading "Dream Big". I needed that then to form a growth mindset and learn anything is possible. I still see that rabbit every morning next to my coffeepot and it inspires me to take on each day with purpose. I love you both and I hope my adulthood makes up for my childhood. At any rate, it's never been a dull moment, right?

To Grandma: as you said in your 103+ years here, "always try your best" and "never give up". That's this book in a nutshell. We miss and love you Gma, but won't ever forget your wisdom you passed down to us.

And to everyone that's played a part in my life and the pages of this book, in my office or out- family, friends, co-workers, and clients, I couldn't have done this without you. Thank you all for your support and guidance and I hope I can give back more than what I've received.

DISCLOSURES

SONG CREDITS

"Ice Ice Baby." Written by Robert Van Winkle (Vanilla Ice), Earthquake, and Mario Johnson. Performed by Vanilla Ice. Released on To the Extreme by SBK Records, 1990. Published by Universal Music Publishing Group. Copyright held by Robert Van Winkle, Earthquake, and Mario Johnson.

"Straight Outta Compton." Written by O'Shea Jackson (Ice Cube), Lorenzo Patterson (MC Ren), and Andre Young (Dr. Dre). Performed by N.W.A. Released on Straight Outta Compton by Ruthless Records, 1988. Published by Universal Music Publishing Group. Copyright held by O'Shea Jackson, Lorenzo Patterson, and Andre Young.

"Jump." Written by Jermaine Dupri. Performed by Kris Kross. Released on Totally Krossed Out by Ruffhouse Records, 1992. Published by EMI Music Publishing. Copyright held by Jermaine Dupri.

"Baby Got Back." Written by Anthony L. Ray (Sir Mix-a-Lot). Performed by Sir Mix-a-Lot. Released on Mack Daddy by Def American Recordings, 1992. Published by Universal Music Publishing Group. Copyright held by Anthony L. Ray.

"Juicy." Written by Christopher Wallace (The Notorious B.I.G.), Sean Combs (Puff Daddy), and James Harris III. Performed by The Notorious B.I.G. Released on Ready to Die by Bad Boy Records, 1994. Published by Warner Chappell Music, Inc. Copyright held by Christopher Wallace, Sean Combs, and James Harris III.

"U Can't Touch This." Written by Stanley Burrell (MC Hammer) and Rick James. Performed by MC Hammer. Released on Please Hammer, Don't Hurt 'Em by Capitol Records, 1990. Published by EMI Music Publishing and Rick James Music. Copyright held by Stanley Burrell and Rick James.

"Fight the Power." Written by Carlton Ridenhour (Chuck D), Hank Shocklee, Eric Sadler, and Keith Shocklee. Performed by Public Enemy. Released on Fear of a Black Planet by Def Jam Recordings, 1990. Published by Universal Music Publishing Group. Copyright held by Carlton Ridenhour, Hank Shocklee, Eric Sadler, and Keith Shocklee.

"Ten Crack Commandments." Written by Christopher Wallace (The Notorious B.I.G.) and Sean Combs (Puff Daddy). Performed by The Notorious B.I.G. Released on Life After Death by Bad Boy Records, 1997. Published by Warner Chappell Music, Inc. and Sean Combs Music. Copyright held by Christopher Wallace and Sean Combs.

"C.R.E.A.M." Written by Robert Diggs (RZA), Gary Grice (GZA), Ol' Dirty Bastard, Russell Jones (Ol' Dirty Bastard), and Clifford Smith (Method Man). Performed by Wu-Tang Clan. Released on Enter the Wu-Tang (36 Chambers) by Loud Records, 1993. Published by EMI Music Publishing. Copyright held by Robert Diggs, Gary Grice, Russell Jones, and Clifford Smith.

"Money Trees." Written by Kendrick Duckworth (Kendrick Lamar), Sounwave (Mark

Anthony Anthony), and Terrence Henderson (TDE). Performed by Kendrick Lamar featuring Jay Rock. Released on good kid, m.A.A.d city by Top Dawg Entertainment, 2012. Published by Universal Music Publishing Group and Top Dawg Entertainment. Copyright held by Kendrick Duckworth, Mark Anthony Anthony, and Terrence Henderson.

"Donald Trump." Written by Malcolm McCormick (Mac Miller). Performed by Mac Miller. Released on Blue Slide Park by Rostrum Records, 2011. Published by Warner Chappell Music, Inc. Copyright held by Malcolm McCormick.

"Mama Said Knock You Out." Written by James Todd Smith (LL Cool J) and Marlon Williams. Performed by LL Cool J. Released on Mama Said Knock You Out by Def Jam and Columbia Records, 1990. Published by Def Jam and Columbia Records. Copyright by Universal Music Corporation, Bridgeport Music Inc., Harlem Music Inc., Jimi Mac Music, Mijac Music, Rubber Band Music, and Universal Music Z Songs.

"Skypager." Written by Q-Tip (Kamaal Fareed), Phife Dawg (Malik Taylor), and Ali Shaheed Muhammad. Performed by A Tribe Called Quest. Released on Midnight Marauders by Jive Records, 1993. Published by Zomba Music Publishers. Copyright held by Q-Tip, Phife Dawg, and Ali Shaheed Muhammad.

"Incarcerated Scarfaces." Written by Corey Woods (Raekwon), Robert Diggs (RZA), and Gary Grice (GZA). Performed by Raekwon. Released on Only Built 4 Cuban Linx... by Loud Records, 1995. Published by Universal Music Publishing Group. Copyright held by Corey Woods, Robert Diggs, and Gary Grice.

"Country Grammar." Written by Cornell Haynes Jr. (Nelly), and Jason Epperson. Performed by Nelly. Released on Country Grammar by Universal Records, 2000. Published by Universal Music Publishing Group. Copyright held by Cornell Haynes Jr. and Jason Epperson.

"So Appalled." Written by Kanye West, Jay-Z, Pusha T, Cyhi the Prynce, and Mike Dean. Performed by Kanye West featuring Jay-Z, Pusha T, and Cyhi the Prynce. Released on My Beautiful Dark Twisted Fantasy by Roc-A-Fella Records, 2010. Published by Universal Music Publishing Group. Copyright held by Kanye West, Jay-Z, Pusha T, Cyhi the Prynce, and Mike Dean.

"Keep Ya Head Up." Written by Tupac Shakur (2Pac), and Deon Evans. Performed by 2Pac. Released on Strictly 4 My N.I.G.G.A.Z. by Interscope Records, 1993. Published by Warner Chappell Music, Inc. and Death Row Publishing. Copyright held by Tupac Shakur and Deon Evans.

"Happy." Written by Pharrell Williams. Performed by Pharrell Williams. Released on G I R L by Columbia Records, 2014. Published by Universal Music Publishing Group. Copyright held by Pharrell Williams.

"Hit 'Em Up." Written by Tupac Shakur (2Pac), and others. Performed by 2Pac. Released as a B-side for the song "How Do U Want It" from the studio album All Eyez on Me by Death Row Records, 1996. Published by Death Row Publishing. Copyright held by Tupac Shakur and collaborators.

"It Was a Good Day." Written by O'Shea Jackson (Ice Cube), DJ Pooh, and others. Performed by Ice Cube. Released on The Predator by Priority Records, 1992. Published by Universal Music Publishing Group and others. Copyright held by O'Shea Jackson and collaborators.

"Can't Tell Me Nothing." Written by Kanye West, DJ Toomp, and others. Performed by Kanye West. Released on 808s & Heartbreak by Roc-A-Fella Records, 2008. Published by Universal Music Publishing Group and others. Copyright held by Kanye West and collaborators.

"The Story of O.J." Written by Shawn Carter (Jay-Z) and others. Performed by Jay-Z. Released on 4:44 by Roc Nation, 2017. Published by Universal Music Publishing Group and others. Copyright held by Shawn Carter and collaborators.

"Diamonds from Sierra Leone." Written by Kanye West, S1 (Symbolic One), and others. Performed by Kanye West. Released on Late Registration by Roc-A-Fella Records, 2005. Published by Universal Music Publishing Group and others. Copyright held by Kanye West and collaborators.

"8 Mile." Written by Eminem (Marshall Mathers), Luis Resto, and others. Performed by Eminem. Released on the 8 Mile soundtrack by Shady Records, 2002. Published by Universal Music Publishing Group and others. Copyright held by Eminem and collaborators.

"Lose Yourself." Written by Eminem (Marshall Mathers), Luis Resto, and Jeff Bass. Performed by Eminem. Released on the 8 Mile soundtrack by Shady Records, 2002. Published by Universal Music Publishing Group and others. Copyright held by Eminem, Luis Resto, and Jeff Bass.

"Hard Knock Life (Ghetto Anthem)." Written by Shawn Carter (Jay-Z), and others. Performed by Jay-Z. Released on Vol. 2... Hard Knock Life by Roc-A-Fella Records, 1998. Published by Universal Music Publishing Group and others. Copyright held by Shawn Carter and collaborators.

"'03 Bonnie & Clyde." Written by Shawn Carter (Jay-Z), Beyoncé Knowles, and others. Performed by Beyoncé featuring Jay-Z. Released on Dangerously in Love by Columbia Records, 2003. Published by Universal Music Publishing Group and others. Copyright held by Shawn Carter, Beyoncé Knowles, and collaborators.

"Run This Town." Written by Shawn Carter (Jay-Z), Rihanna Fenty, Kanye West, and others. Performed by Jay-Z featuring Rihanna and Kanye West. Released on The

Blueprint 3 by Roc Nation, 2009. Published by Universal Music Publishing Group and others. Copyright held by Shawn Carter, Rihanna Fenty, Kanye West, and collaborators.

"Don't Sweat the Technique." Written by William Griffin Jr. (Rakim) and Eric B. (Eric Barrier). Performed by Eric B. and Rakim. Released on Don't Sweat the Technique by Uni Records, 1992. Published by Universal Music Publishing Group. Copyright held by William Griffin Jr. and Eric Barrier.

"Wanna Be a Baller." Written by Troy B. Hightower (Lil' Troy), and others. Performed by Lil' Troy. Released on Sittin' Fat Down South by Short Stop Records, 1998. Published by Short Stop Publishing. Copyright held by Troy B. Hightower and collaborators.

"Started from the Bottom." Written by Aubrey Graham (Drake), Noah Shebib (40), and others. Performed by Drake. Released on Nothing Was the Same by Young Money Entertainment, 2013. Published by Universal Music Publishing Group and others. Copyright held by Aubrey Graham and collaborators.

"R.I.C.O." Written by Robert Williams (Meek Mill), Aubrey Graham (Drake), and others. Performed by Meek Mill featuring Drake. Released on Dreams Worth More Than Money by Maybach Music Group and Atlantic Records, 2015. Published by Universal Music Publishing Group and others. Copyright held by Robert Williams, Aubrey Graham, and collaborators.

"All I Do Is Win." Written by Khaled Khaled (DJ Khaled), Faheem Najm (T-Pain), Christopher Bridges (Ludacris), William Roberts II (Rick Ross), Calvin Broadus Jr. (Snoop Dogg), and others. Performed by DJ Khaled featuring T-Pain, Ludacris, Rick Ross, and Snoop Dogg. Released on Victory by We the Best Music Group and Koch Records, 2010. Published by Universal Music Publishing Group and others. Copyright held by Khaled Khaled, Faheem Najm, Christopher Bridges, William Roberts II, Calvin Broadus Jr., and collaborators.

"U.O.E.N.O." Written by Rocko, Nayvadius Wilburn (Future), William Roberts II (Rick Ross), and others. Performed by Rocko featuring Future and Rick Ross. Released on Gift of Gab by Epic Records, 2013. Published by Universal Music Publishing Group and others. Copyright held by Rocko, Nayvadius Wilburn, William Roberts II, and collaborators.

"No Sleep Till Brooklyn." Written by Michael Diamond (Mike D), Adam Horovitz (Ad-Rock), Adam Yauch (MCA), and Rick Rubin. Performed by Beastie Boys. Released on Licensed to Ill by Def Jam Recordings, 1986. Published by Universal Music Publishing Group and others. Copyright held by Michael Diamond, Adam Horovitz, Adam Yauch, and Rick Rubin.

"Walk This Way." Written by Steven Tyler, Joe Perry, and others. Performed by

Run-D.M.C. featuring Aerosmith. Released on Raising Hell by Profile Records, 1986. Published by Universal Music Publishing Group and others. Copyright held by Steven Tyler, Joe Perry, and collaborators.

"99 Problems." Written by Shawn Carter (Jay-Z), Rick Rubin, and others. Performed by Jay-Z. Released on The Black Album by Roc-A-Fella Records, 2003. Published by Universal Music Publishing Group and others. Copyright held by Shawn Carter, Rick Rubin, and collaborators.

"Mo Money Mo Problems." Written by Christopher Wallace (The Notorious B.I.G.), Sean Combs (Puff Daddy), Mason Betha (Mase), and others. Performed by The Notorious B.I.G. featuring Puff Daddy and Mase. Released on Life After Death by Bad Boy Records, 1997. Published by Warner Chappell Music, Inc. and Sean Combs Music. Copyright held by Christopher Wallace, Sean Combs, Mason Betha, and collaborators.

"How to Rob." Written by Curtis Jackson (50 Cent), and others. Performed by 50 Cent. Released on Power of the Dollar (later re-released on Guess Who's Back?) by Columbia Records, 2000. Published by Universal Music Publishing Group and others. Copyright held by Curtis Jackson and collaborators.

"Thrift Shop." Written by Macklemore (Ben Haggerty), Ryan Lewis, and Wanz (Michael Wansley). Performed by Macklemore & Ryan Lewis featuring Wanz. Released on The Heist by Macklemore LLC and Ryan Lewis LLC, 2012. Published by Macklemore LLC, Ryan Lewis LLC, and Universal Music Publishing Group. Copyright held by Macklemore, Ryan Lewis, and Wanz.

"In Da Club." Written by Curtis Jackson (50 Cent), Dr. Dre (Andre Young), and Mike Elizondo. Performed by 50 Cent. Released on Get Rich or Die Tryin' by Interscope Records, 2003. Published by Universal Music Publishing Group and others. Copyright held by Curtis Jackson, Dr. Dre, and Mike Elizondo.

"Moment of Clarity." Written by Shawn Carter (Jay-Z), and others. Performed by Jay-Z. Released on The Black Album by Roc-A-Fella Records, 2003. Published by Universal Music Publishing Group and others. Copyright held by Shawn Carter and collaborators.

"Bad and Boujee." Written by Quavo (Quavious Marshall), Offset (Kiari Cephus), Takeoff (Kirsnick Ball), Symere Woods (Lil Uzi Vert), and others. Performed by Migos featuring Lil Uzi Vert. Released on Culture by Quality Control Music and 300 Entertainment, 2017. Published by Universal Music Publishing Group and others. Copyright held by Quavo, Offset, Takeoff, Lil Uzi Vert, and collaborators.

"Self Care." Written by Malcolm McCormick (Mac Miller) and others. Performed by Mac Miller. Released on Swimming by Warner Bros. Records, 2018. Published by Warner Chappell Music, Inc. and others. Copyright held by Malcolm McCormick and collaborators.

"Good Vibrations." Written by Mark Wahlberg (Marky Mark), Donnie Wahlberg, and others. Performed by Marky Mark and the Funky Bunch. Released on Music for the People by Interscope Records, 1991. Published by Universal Music Publishing Group and others. Copyright held by Mark Wahlberg, Donnie Wahlberg, and collaborators.

REFERENCES

Pg. 8 Lonsdorf, K. (2023, July 11). 50 years ago, teenagers partied in the Bronx and gave rise to hip-hop. NPR. https://www.npr.org/2023/07/11/1186407223/50-years-ago-teenagers-partied-in-the-bronx-and-gave-rise-to-hip-hop

Pg. 8 Nix, G. J. (2023, August 21). 50 Years: Quantifying Hip-Hop's official golden age beyond the stage - CultureBanx. CultureBanx. https://www.culturebanx.com/cbx-daily/50-years-quantifying-hip-hops-official-golden-age-beyond-the-stage/#:~:text=It's%20already%20difficult%20enough%20to%20quantify%20hip,we%20look%20at%20Jay%2DZ%2C%20Diddy%2C%20KanYe%20West%2C

Pg. 14 What is the Most Sampled Drum Beat Ever? (2023, January 25). Tracklib.com. https://www.tracklib.com/blog/most-sampled-drum-beat

Pg. 18 Hop, R. H. (2020, May 1). Once-Ballin' rappers who went broke. Ranker. https://www.ranker.com/list/rappers-who-went-broke/ranker-hip-hop

Pg. 18 Rodgers, J. (n.d.-a). How MC Hammer went from bankruptcy and losing it all to becoming one of Silicon Valley's most respected tech investors - AfroTech. AfroTech. https://afrotech.com/mc-hammer-investments

Pg. 27 Frequently asked questions (FAQs) – Credit counseling. (2024, May 1). https://www.justice.gov/ust/frequently-asked-questions-faqs-credit-counseling

Pg. 27 Graham, D. A. (2024, November 22). The Cases Against Trump: A guide. The Atlantic. https://www.theatlantic.com/ideas/archive/2024/11/donald-trump-legal-cases-charges/675531/

Pg. 27 Long, C., Balsamo, M., Sisak, M. R., & Jalonick, M. C. (2024, July 18). Investigations: Unraveling the attempted assassination of Donald Trump | AP News. AP News. https://apnews.com/article/trump-shooting-rally-a1bcbaa4a604e09be8cc22893751895b

Pg. 27 Murphy, J. S. &. M. (2024, November 6). Donald Trump projected to pull-off historic White House comeback. https://www.bbc.com/news/articles/c62l5zdv7zko

Pg. 37 Complex. (2011, April 25). The official history of the Nike Air Yeezy. Complex. https://www.complex.com/sneakers/a/complex/the-official-history-of-the-nike-air-yeezy

Pg. 38 Tfl. (2022, November 8). Kanye West's Yeezy Venture is a Multi-Billion Dollar Business and Still Growing. The Fashion Law. https://www.thefashionlaw.com/kanye-wests-yeezy-venture-is-worth-1-billion-and-growing/

Pg. 38 Santana, D., Kish, M., & Reuter, D. (2023, October 27). Adidas cut ties with Ye a year ago, but the controversies keep coming. Here's a history of the brand's decade-long relationship with Kanye West. Business Insider. https://www.businessinsider.com/kanye-wests-turbulent-9-year-history-with-adidas-2022-11

Pg. 38 Voytko-Best, L. (2024, February 20). Here's why Kanye West dropped off the Forbes billionaires list. Forbes. https://www.forbes.com/sites/lisettevoytko/2023/04/05/heres-why-kanye-west-dropped-off-the-forbes-billionaires-list/

Pg. 40 Corney, C. (n.d.). Do ostriches really bury their head in the sand? https://www.sciencefocus.com/nature/do-ostriches-really-bury-their-head-in-the-sand

Pg. 40 https://www.fool.com/money/credit-cards/articles/wild-purchases-people-actually-made-with-the-amex-black-card/#:~:text=Mansions%2C%20jets%2C%20and%20cars,knowledge%20of%20their%20spending%20patterns.%22

Pg. 41 Clark, A. (n.d.). escenic. The Telegraph. https://www.telegraph.co.uk/culture/art/art-news/11985399/Modiglianis-Nu-Couche-sold-for-record-113-million.html

Pg. 44 Oü, C. S. (2023, September 3). Rick Ross Jewelry: inside the $1.5 million dollar face chain. Icecartel. https://icecartel.com/blogs/news/rick-ross-jewelry?srsltid=AfmBOopgGmMe7hTMO027W3hf_ufgAtLY8p979DVoygC8P-_UGqRS7PLa

Pg. 47 DeNicola, L. (2023, April 16). What is a good credit score? Experian. https://www.experian.com/blogs/ask-experian/credit-education/score-basics/what-is-a-good-credit-score/

Pg. 51 Jay-Z. (n.d.). Forbes. https://www.forbes.com/profile/jay-z/

Pg. 52 Beattie, A. (2024, November 5). Who coined the term 'Entrepreneur?' Investopedia. https://www.investopedia.com/ask/answers/08/origin-of-entrepreneur.asp#:~:text=Entrepreneur%20is%20a%20French%20word,businessmen%20was%20a%20serious%20flaw

Pg. 54 Michael Jordan career shots missed | StatMuse. (n.d.). StatMuse. https://www.statmuse.com/nba/ask/michael-jordan-career-shots-missed

Pg. 58 Jesse's Journey. (n.d.). Jesse Itzler. https://jesseitzler.com/pages/jesses-journey?srsltid=AfmBOoo9oGKcdxXvkgBwB2WCcZBqKQnOGGGqp0sIg6jgR0wTWOG359Za

Pg. 58 Ocho, A. (2023, September 19). Atlanta Hawks owner tells inspiring story about 50 cent interning for him, 50 confirms it's '100 percent true.' Complex. https://www.complex.com/music/a/alex-ocho/50-cent-interning-atlanta-hawks-owner-story-jesse-itzler

Pg. 58 Scipioni, J. (2020, April 20). This founder had to take a loan for Yankees tickets in the '90s—now he's a multi-millionaire: "Bet on yourself." CNBC. https://www.cnbc.com/2020/04/18/multimillionaire-jesse-itzler-bet-on-yourself.html

Pg. 59 Bernstein, A. (2002, December 9). Alphabet City alums soar after selling firm to SFX. Sports Business Journal. https://www.sportsbusinessjournal.com/Journal/Issues/2002/12/09/SFX-A-Sports-Business-Epic/Alphabet-City-Alums-Soar-After-Selling-Firm-To-SFX.aspx

Pg. 59 Bernstein, A. (2002, December 9). Alphabet City alums soar after selling firm to SFX. Sports Business Journal. https://www.sportsbusinessjournal.com/Journal/Issues/2002/12/09/SFX-A-Sports-Business-Epic/Alphabet-City-Alums-Soar-After-Selling-Firm-To-SFX.aspx

Pg. 60 Magazine, M. S. (2023, July 25). 12 Life-Changing Ways to Create Your Own Luck. MSP Success. https://mspsuccess.com/2022/12/12-life-changing-ways-to-create-your-own-luck/

Pg. 61 Fontevecchia, A. (2015, April 22). Billionaires Tony Ressler and Sara Blakely snatch Atlanta Hawks for $730M. Forbes. https://www.forbes.com/sites/afontevecchia/2015/04/22/billionaires-tony-ressler-and-sara-blakely-snatch-atlanta-hawks-for-850m-reports/

Pg. 62 Big Daddy Kane | Justin BUA | Legends | Hip Hop - Justinbua. (2017, August 25). Justinbua. https://justinbua.com/products/big-daddy-kane?srsltid=AfmBOorEsFz6vGB-UkBZIKsVs6C8urZugJCttfFflvqFthRWXZZ6596K

Pg. 64 Rodgers, J. (n.d.). Lil Wayne once had $14M in tax debt and Jay-Z came through — "That man helped me with my taxes" - AfroTech. AfroTech. https://afrotech.com/lil-wayne-tax-debt

Pg. 68 Cooper, A. (2023, May 28). In Shangri-La with music producer Rick Rubin | 60 Minutes. CBS News. https://www.cbsnews.com/news/rick-rubin-60-minutes-transcript-2023-05-28/

Pg. 69 Deane, M. T. (2024, June 1). Top 6 reasons new businesses fail. Investopedia. https://www.investopedia.com/financial-edge/1010/top-6-reasons-new-businesses-fail.aspx#:~:text=Data%20from%20the%20BLS%20shows,to%2015%20years%20or%20more

Pg. 70 Solomon, B. (2014, May 29). It's official: Apple adds Dr. Dre with $3 billion beats deal. Forbes. https://www.forbes.com/sites/briansolomon/2014/05/28/apple-brings-dr-dre-on-board-with-official-3-billion-beats-deal/

Pg. 71 Srinivasan, H. (2023, November 25). Jay-Z's Net Worth and Businesses, as the Rapper Gives Rare Interview With CBS. Investopedia. https://www.investopedia.com/jay-z-net-worth-and-businesses-8405817

Pg. 75 Hershman-Jones, A. J., & Hershman-Jones, A. J. (2023, November 20). 50 Cent tells how he blew $470 million and went bankrupt. Supercar Blondie. https://supercarblondie.com/50-cent-blew-470-million-fortune-bankrupt/

Pg. 75 Lane, B. (2023, February 7). 50 Cent's debut album "Get Rich or Die Tryin'" turns 20. This is the story of how it was made, from recording in a safe house to hitting No. 1 and touring on a bulletproof bus. Business Insider. https://www.businessinsider.com/50-cent-get-rich-die-tryin-20-anniversary-inside-story-2023-01#:~:text=50%20Cent's%20back%20story%20is,arrested%20for%20carrying%20a%20gun.

Pg. 76 5 MOST FAMOUS RAPPERS WHO ALSO TRAIN BOXING. (2023, September 17). BOXROPE®. https://boxrope.com/blogs/boxing/5-most-famous-rappers-who-also-train-boxing#:~:text=But%20before%20Curtis%20Jackson%20became,to%20the%20sport%20of%20boxing.

Pg. 76 50 Cent: The Life of a Hunted Man | Rolling Stone Music. (n.d.). https://web.archive.org/web/20110523003637/http://www.rollingstone.com/music/news/50-cent-the-life-of-a-hunted-man-20030403

Pg. 77 Moore, S. (2023, November 28). 50 Cent reveals first purchase after $1M Dr. Dre & Eminem deal. HipHopDX. https://hiphopdx.com/news/50-cent-first-purchase-dr-dre-eminem-record-deal-1-million

Pg. 77 Hattenstone, S. (2020, May 15). 50 Cent on love, cash and bankruptcy: 'When there are setbacks, there will be get-backs.' The Guardian. https://www.theguardian.com/music/2020/may/04/50-cent-on-love-cash-and-bankruptcy-when-there-are-setbacks-there-will-be-get-backs

Pg. 77 Elibert, M. (2024, May 29). 50 Cent explains purchasing Mike Tyson's 52-Room house in 2003. HipHopDX. https://hiphopdx.com/news/id.65224/title.50-cent-mike-tyson-mansion

Pg. 77 Yahoo is part of the Yahoo family of brands. (n.d.-b). https://finance.yahoo.com/news/50-cent-once-revealed-earned-181856987.html

Pg. 77 Yahoo is part of the Yahoo family of brands. (n.d.). https://finance.yahoo.com/news/50-cent-made-estimated-100m-230731066.html

Pg. 78 50 cent bankruptcy: by the numbers | ABI. (n.d.). https://www.abi.org/feed-item/50-cent-bankruptcy-by-the-numbers-0

Pg. 78 Blistein, J. (2022, November 23). 50 Cent's Spent $23 Million on Legal Fees —

And There's More Coming With Penis Enhancement Suit. Rolling Stone. https://www.rollingstone.com/music/music-news/50-cents-23-million-lawyers-legal-fees-1234636371/

Pg. 82 Nededog, J. (2015, August 5). 50 Cent admits he spends $108,000 per month on things like grooming, gardening and clothing. Business Insider. https://www.businessinsider.com/50-cent-bankruptcy-monthly-expenses-2015-8#:~:text=50%20Cent%20admits%20he%20spends,like%20grooming%2C%20gardening%20and%20clothing

Pg. 83 Holloway, D. (2018, October 11). Variety. Variety. https://variety.com/2018/tv/news/50-cent-signs-massive-multi-series-starz-deal-exclusive-1202976593/

Pg. 83 Rouse, I. (2017, July 18). 50 Cent sells Effen Vodka Stake for $60 million USD. Hypebeast. https://hypebeast.com/2017/7/50-cent-sells-effen-vodka-stake-60-million-usd

Pg. 83 Saponara, M. (2024, May 16). 50 Cent's Final Lap Tour Makes History, Becoming Only Third Rap Trek Ever to Cross $100M. Billboard. https://www.billboard.com/music/chart-beat/50-cent-final-lap-tour-grosses-100-million-rap-history-1235684967/

Pg. 84 Cepf, L. G. T., & Grace, M. (2024, July 22). The 28/36 rule explained for mortgage borrowers. Business Insider. https://www.businessinsider.com/personal-finance/mortgages/28-36-rule-mortgages#:~:text=The%2028%2F36%20rule%20is,monthly%20income%20on%20housing%20expenses.

Pg. 85 Show, M. G. (2024, September 13). What is the 20/3/8 Rule for Car Affordability? | Money Guy. Money Guy. https://moneyguy.com/article/20-3-8-rule/#:~:text=Your%20monthly%20loan%20payment%2C%20or,monthly%20car%20payment(s).

Pg 86. Bieber, C., JD. (2024, November 20). Revealing divorce statistics in 2024. Forbes Advisor. https://www.forbes.com/advisor/legal/divorce/divorce-statistics/#:~:text=Key%20Divorce%20Statistics%20in%202024%20In%202022%2C%20a,the%20course%20of%20each%20year%20than%20get%20divorced.

Pg. 91 Today, U. (2023, August 7). Sealed first generation iPod bought as a Christmas gift in 2001 sells for $29,000. USA TODAY. https://www.usatoday.com/story/tech/news/2023/08/03/original-ipod-sealed-sold-rally/70518816007/

Pg. 92 Greenburg, Z. O. (2021, June 28). Dr. Dre's $3 Billion Monster: The Secret History of Beats. Forbes. https://www.forbes.com/sites/zackomalleygreenburg/2018/03/08/dr-dres-3-billion-monster-the-secret-history-of-beats-3-kings-book-excerpt/

Pg. 92 History : i.am.angel foundation. (n.d.). https://www.iamangelfoundation.org/about/history/

Pg. 94 Staff, A. (2014, June 12). Samsung endorser LeBron James made a reported $30M from Apple's Beats buy. AppleInsider. https://appleinsider.com/articles/14/06/12/samsung-endorser-lebron-james-made-a-reported-30m-from-apples-beats-buy

Pg. 99 Brown, A. (2023, November 9). Here's how Drake got his private plane for free. Atlanta Black Star. https://atlantablackstar.com/2023/11/09/drake-private-plane/

Pg. 100 Sauer, M., & Ward, M. (2024, June 9). Warren Buffett says this public speaking class changed his life—4 tips from the course. CNBC. https://www.cnbc.com/2024/06/09/warren-buffett-says-public-speaking-class-changed-his-life-what-he-learned.html#:~:text=He%20enrolled%20in%20a%20%24100,Influence%20People%E2%80%9D%20and%20other%20bestsellers.&text=%E2%80%B3%5BThe%20class%5D%20certainly%20had,success%2C%E2%80%9D%20Buffett%20told%20Segal.

Pg. 100 Warner, B. (2017, October 12). Floyd Mayweather keeps $123 million cash in his checking account | Celebrity net worth. Celebrity Net Worth. https://www.celebritynetworth.com/articles/entertainment-articles/floyd-mayweather-keeps-123-million-cash-checking-account/

Pg. 101 Deposit Insurance FAQs | FDIC. (n.d.). https://www.fdic.gov/resources/deposit-insurance/faq#:~:text=The%20standard%20deposit%20insurance%20coverage,held%20at%20the%20same%20bank.

Pg. 104 Vanguard by the numbers. (n.d.). Vanguard. https://corporate.vanguard.com/content/corporatesite/us/en/corp/who-we-are/sets-us-apart/facts-and-figures.html#:~:text=Vanguard%20is%20one%20of%20the,%2C%20institutions%2C%20and%20financial%20professionals.

Pg. 108 Cummings-Grady, M. (2022, July 20). French Montana accuses record labels of profiting off rappers' deaths with life insurance policies. Complex. https://www.complex.com/music/a/mack/french-montana-accuses-record-labels-profiting-off-rappers-deaths-life-insurance-policies

Pg. 110 Rockefellers vs. Vanderbilts: The Importance of Estate Planning. (n.d.). Dispute. https://getdispute.com/guide/rockefellers-vs-vanderbilts-the-importance-of-estate-planning

Pg. 112 Britannica money. (2024, November 22). https://www.britannica.com/money/Standard-Oil

Pg. 112 Writer, S. (2021, October 4). Rockefellers v. Vanderbilts: Estate Planning Lessons | Trust & Will. Trust & Will. https://trustandwill.com/learn/rockefellers-vs-vanderbilts?srsltid=AfmBOooANH-ap4haiNCS6YIOoEJ7vRRHmSyUxgvsiG3_9AQUXF7Yl9E

Pg. 113 Rodgers, J. (n.d.-c). Lil Wayne once had $14M in tax debt and Jay-Z came through — "That man helped me with my taxes" - AfroTech. AfroTech. https://afrotech.com/lil-wayne-tax-debt

Pg. 115 Hodder, Catherine. (2022, December 22). What Rappers Can Teach You about Estate Planning. FindLaw. www.findlaw.com/legalblogs/estate-planning/what-rappers-can-teach-you-about-estate-planning.

Pg. 116 The tragic death of Migos rapper Takeoff: a Wake-Up call for young adults to plan their estates. (2024, August 20). JD Supra. https://www.jdsupra.com/legalnews/the-tragic-death-of-migos-rapper-4071759/

Pg. 117 Lw. (2023, October 4). Tupac Shakur Net Worth: What is Tupac's estate worth today? MARCA. https://www.marca.com/en/lifestyle/celebrity-net-worth/2023/10/04/651d97c422601d604c8b45e7.html

Pg. 117 Brown, P. (2024, February 1). VIBE.com. VIBE.com. https://www.vibe.com/news/entertainment/nate-doggs-wife-children-split-estate-payout-1234846529/

Pg. 117 Erskine, M. F., JD. (2024, January 19). The Battle for Prince's Estate: unending conflict, legal drama and lessons for family business. Forbes. https://www.forbes.com/sites/matthewerskine/2024/01/17/the-battle-for-princes-estate-unending-conflict-legal-drama-and-lessons-for-family-business/#:~:text=The%20Battle%20For%20Prince's%20Estate,And%20Lessons%20For%20Family%20Business

Pg. 117 Snowden, D. (2019, March 11). Bob Marley's legacy mired in estate battle - Los Angeles Times. Los Angeles Times. https://www.latimes.com/archives/la-xpm-1989-02-04-ca-1568-story.html

Pg. 118 Jimi Hendrix: A Cautionary Tale for Estate Planning | Doane & Doane. (2024, March 28). https://www.doaneanddoane.com/the-late-jimi-hendrix-a-cautionary-tale-for-estate-planning

Pg. 120 McIlveen, A. (2019, February 10). Valid Last Will & Testament NC. McIlveen Family Law Firm. https://mcilveenfamilylaw.com/executing-a-valid-will/

Pg. 135 What is Intellectual Property (IP)? (n.d.). https://www.wipo.int/about-ip/en/

Pg. 136 Robinson, K. (2023, March 7). Metro Boomin sells portion of publishing Catalog to Shamrock for close to $70M. Billboard. https://www.billboard.com/pro/metro-boomin-sold-publishing-catalog-shamrock-price/

Pg. 136 Sullivan, M. (2024, August 12). Michael Jackson takes control of the Beatles' publishing rights. HISTORY. https://www.history.com/this-day-in-history/michael-jackson-takes-control-of-the-beatles-publishing-rights

Pg.137 About - the giving pledge. (n.d.). Giving Pledge. https://givingpledge.org/about

Pg.137 Shawn Carter Foundation. (2023, April 13). Shawn Carter Foundation | Our Scholars. https://shawncartersf.com/about-alumni/

Pg.138 The Book of HOV: A celebration of the life and work of Shawn "JAY-Z" Carter | Brooklyn Public Library. (2023, July 14). https://www.bklynlibrary.org/exhibitions/book-hov

Pg.138 About : i.am.angel foundation. (n.d.). https://www.iamangelfoundation.org/about/

Pg. 139 History, A. C.-. I. Q. &. F. |. (2021, February 9). Andrew Carnegie - Industry, Quotes & Fortune | HISTORY. HISTORY. https://www.history.com/topics/19th-century/andrew-carnegie

Pg. 140 Elibert, M. (2023, July 16). Jay-Z's Shawn Carter Foundation raises $20 million at Black-Tie NYC Gala. Complex. https://www.complex.com/music/a/markelibert/jay-z-shawn-carter-foundation-anniversary

Pg. 141 Rapper Jay-Z wins award for 'Water for Life' campaign involving UN. (2007, November 14). UN News. https://news.un.org/en/story/2007/11/239602

Pg. 141 Stone, R. (2018, June 25). Jay-Z performs at Carnegie Hall, parties at 40/40 Club. Rolling Stone. https://www.rollingstone.com/music/music-lists/jay-z-performs-at-carnegie-hall-parties-at-40-40-club-10296/

Pg. 141 Robertson, J. (2018, June 25). Diddy, Jay-Z, More Donate to Katrina Cause. Rolling Stone. https://www.rollingstone.com/music/music-news/diddy-jay-z-more-donate-to-katrina-cause-112811/

Pg. 141 Yabut, R. (2023, October 6). Jimmy Iovine and Dr. Dre give $70 million to create new academy at USC. USC Today. https://today.usc.edu/jimmy-iovine-and-dr-dre-give-70-million-to-create-new-academy-at-usc/

Pg. 141 Ferreiro, L. (2012, October 4). Variety. Variety. https://variety.com/2012/film/markets-festivals/queen-latifah-helping-educate-the-next-generation-1118059855/

Pg. 142 Essence, B. (2020, October 30). The 2008 Keep A Child Alive's Black Ball. Essence. https://www.essence.com/news/2008-keep-child-alives-black-ball/

Pg. 142 The Ludacris Foundation. (2021, April 6). LudaCares® Programs | The Ludacris Foundation. The Ludacris Foundation | Helping Youth Help Themselves. https://theludacrisfoundation.org/pillars/ludacares/

Pg. 142 Reports, S., & Reports, S. (2015, August 6). Missy Elliott: The Heavy-Hittin'

Donor. BORGEN. https://www.borgenmagazine.com/missy-elliott-heavy-hittn-donor/#:~:text=Elliott's%20participation%20in%20the%20campaign,research%20in%20alleviating%20HIV%2FAIDS.

Pg. 143 Grein, P. (2023, June 27). Lil Wayne to be Named a BMI Icon at 2023 BMI R&B/Hip-Hop Awards. Billboard. https://www.billboard.com/music/awards/lil-wayne-bmi-icon-2023-bmi-rb-hip-hop-awards-1235362604/

Pg. 143 bChesna. (2009, January 13). Lil Wayne donates $200,000 to Childhood Park. HipHopDX. https://hiphopdx.com/news/id.8402/title.lil-wayne-donates-200000-to-childhood-park

Pg. 143 Bet. (2011, November 20). Lil Wayne, Birdman, and Slim host 16th Annual Turkey Giveaway. BET. https://www.bet.com/article/ks65i1/lil-wayne-birdman-and-slim-host-annual-turkey-giveaway

Pg. 143 Newport, K. (2017, October 3). Rick Ross buys Evander Holyfield's 109-Room mansion in Georgia. Bleacher Report. https://bleacherreport.com/articles/1933190-rick-ross-buys-evander-holyfields-109-room-mansion-in-georgia

Pg. 143 Staff, X. (2007, November 2). Rick Ross to Hand out Thanksgiving Turkeys in the Miami Community, Help Launch the Hip-Hop Grub Spot. XXL Mag. https://www.xxlmag.com/rick-ross-to-hand-out-thanksgiving-turkeys-in-the-miami-community-help-launch-the-hip-hop-grub-spot/

Pg. 143 Cummings-Grady, M. (2023, October 3). See Everything Drake spent $400,000 on gifts to fans during It's All A Blur tour. XXL Mag. https://www.xxlmag.com/drake-money-gifts-fans-its-all-a-blur-tour/

Pg. 143 Chuba, K. (2018, February 16). Variety. Variety. https://variety.com/2018/music/news/drake-gives-away-one-million-dollars-gods-plan-video-1202702561/

Pg. 143 Polacek, S. (2022, March 24). Drake donates $1M in bitcoin to LeBron James Family Foundation. Bleacher Report. https://bleacherreport.com/articles/10030706-drake-donates-1m-in-bitcoin-to-lebron-james-family-foundation

ABOUT THE AUTHOR

Drew Boyer is an experienced financial expert and a CERTIFIED FINANCIAL PLANNER® with over two decades of experience helping individuals and families navigate their financial journeys. Raised in Ohio, Drew's upbringing shaped his values of hard work, financial responsibility, and entrepreneurship, lessons that he now imparts to his clients and readers alike.

A passionate advocate for financial literacy, Drew blends his expertise in personal finance with his deep love for hip-hop culture, using the lessons learned from both to educate and inspire. From witnessing the rise of hip-hop in the golden age to overcoming his own financial struggles, Drew's life story mirrors many of the triumphs and pitfalls found in both the financial world and the music industry.

Through his unique perspective, Drew has transformed his challenges into teaching moments, creating a relatable, engaging approach to financial education. His book, Hip Hop X Finance, combines iconic hip-hop references with practical financial advice, delivering money lessons in an entertaining and accessible way.

When Drew isn't helping clients achieve their financial goals, he enjoys traveling to spend time with his family on both sides of the Atlantic, staying active outdoors, and playing or watching live music.